HOOLIFAN

30 YEARS OF HURT

MARTIN KING
AND MARTIN KNIGHT

MAINSTREAM
PUBLISHING

EDINBURGH AND LONDON

First published in Great Britain in 1999 by
MAINSTREAM PUBLISHING COMPANY (EDINBURGH) LTD
7 Albany Street
Edinburgh EH1 3UG

ISBN 9781840181746

Reprinted, 2001, 2002, 2003, 2004, 2006, 2008

A catalogue record for this book is available from the British Library

Printed and bound in Great Britain by
CPI Cox & Wyman, Reading, RG1 8EX

In memory of my dad. A fan of all sports who loved nothing better than to take me along with him. A real gentleman and true father and friend. God bless.

Contents

Acknowledgements

Martin King would like to thank: Martin Knight, his wife Val for the cups of tea and the children Michelle, Billy, Zoe, Daisy and Joe for the entertainment; Stuart and Jimmy Craig for kick-starting the project with their enthusiasm; Stuart for the research; Dawn and Robert Bunker for trusting me with a computer; John King for his unswerving support; Michelle Perry; Mandy, my wife, and the kids Kortney and Rory-Ben for being so understanding; Denise and Jeff; my brother Alan, Hazel, Sophie, Emily and Lucy for their encouragement; my Mum who told me not to be so daft; and the following people who one way or another shaped my football-going days: Bobby Reader, Peter Marney, Danny Smith, Ida and Jack, Steve Woodley, Pear Brewley, Martin, Steve and David Ballard, Steve Whiting, Steve Watkins, Mickey Potter, Tass, the Ginger twins, Sol, Seamus, Tony Aldworth, Jeff Hack, Chimpey Stockley, Micky Beard, Peg and Ted, Dave Thurston, Keith Perland, Dave Perks, Susan and Deb, Ravindra Saravanamuto and all the Pollards Hill gang, Peter Stevens, Brian Wilkes, Maisie, Johnny Irish, Peter Clark, Colin Bourner, Kevin Burden, Dougie Ayres, Dave Metis, Sammy Hance, Mal and Coe, Tony and Denise, Uncle Patsy, Lyons, Michelle and Lisa, Jaffa, Danny Peacock, John and Sally Bloomfield, Dennis Price, Andy Till, Nan, Grandad, Tiger Lyons, Emmy and Winnie, Linda and Bill, Leonard Hance, Davey Small, Steve King, Micky Wheeler and his red setter, Terry Robson, Steve Prentice, Dave Griffin, Martin Thoust, Kenny Aird, Terry and

Micky Coates, Steve Harris, Richard, Amey, Elliot and Grant Millett, Stewart Merrill of Sheffield, Vinny, Eccles, Babsy, Skitzy, Nashy, Dawn and Andy Duncan, Dave Kinshett, Roy and Bruce, Bill with no coat and his sidekicks Les and Andrew, Barry and Julie, Anthony Dillon, Les Ward, Danny and Jackie Smith, Peter and George Clark, Johnny Dixey, Sian and Lee, Danny and Robert, Mickey Ford, Ally Mclean, Mark Banks, Matt and Lee, Ian Cooper, Alex Mac, Christian Leiframilch and Mavis, Len Aherne, Jimmy Barrs, Trevor Hill, Sharpey, Micky Brown, Stephen, Peter and Tony Brown, Stewart Gee, Alan Gadd, Sarge, Glen Williams, Micky Wragg, Eddie, Barry Coles, Rusty Munden, Joe Nelson, Ginger Bill, Mike from Manchester, Muscles, Chris Tudenham, Mark Cator, Kev Sweeney, Puncho, Mark Lyons, Freddie, Helen, Billy, Joe Harley, Scottish Jimmy Wilson, Big Les, Dainton, Big Bill, Brentford Pete, Gardner, Caz, Swallow, Icky, Time Warp Terry Knowles, Geordie Phil, Melvyn, John the Greek, Mick, Pete the Feet, Longways, Paul Lyons, Theo, Bodger, Barney, Whitney, Zola, Copper, Andy, Mark Johnson, Paddy, Fonzie, Tommy Tindall, John Goff, John the Horse, Charlie and everyone else I have for the minute forgotten. Finally, a big thank you to all the birds I've ever shagged, too numerous to mention.

Martin Knight would like to dedicate the book to Eamonn Devaney – old friend, died young – and would like to thank: Terry and Atty Knowles, Mick Woodham, Tony Jones, Kevin, Barry and Peter Merchant, Black Pete Harrison, Chris and Derek Mallows, Clive Aldridge, Alan Sleuman, Paul Fletcher, Tony Miller, Clive Fentum, Steve Fisher, Nicky and Marcus Wade, Bernie Fauld, Dave Pink, Mark Reynolds, Gary Allam, Terry Leonard, Billy Owen, Peter and Mike Bromley, Andy Clarke, Glen Connett, Kirk Stevens, Roy Browes, Dave Williams, Gavin Harkness, Micky Trent, Black John, Tony and Nigel from Edenbridge, Geoff from Hounslow, Dave and Peter Goodsell, Pommy, Woody, Jimmy Ryan, Punky Al, Eccles, Babs, Big Anthony, Jointy, Kevin, Eddie, Alan Hudson, Lofty, Micky Greenaway, John King, Phil Lattimore, Dog, Lianne and Chris Collis, Paul Collis and Geoff, Andy Fellowes, Ian Macleay, Gary Nash, Andy Hall, John Masterson, Paul Hearne and Paul Hearne, Willie, John Taylor, Vic Ware, Billy and Steve Claridge, Bucko, Ian Cox, Sean Wickens, Bob Burns, Tom Sweeney, Steve from Brixton, Danny, Akim and Mark from York, Tony Brand, Derby Steve, Crix, Jim the Builder and anyone else who contributed to this book in any way.

Introduction by John King

I was in the crush of bodies outside Stamford Bridge with my dad, queuing up to see Chelsea play Southampton in 1970, about to watch my first live football match, when the thunder of clapping and the roar of 'ENGLAND' filled the air. The sound came from the other side of a massive wall rising up inside the ground, from under a small metal roof. It was urgent and powerful, with a hard, threatening edge. I felt the excitement race across my skin as the chant was repeated four or five times before stopping dead. I had goosepimples. Still do, all these years later, as I remember the moment when I realised that going to football was about so much more than twenty-two men kicking a ball around a patch of grass. I asked Dad why the crowd were singing 'England' when it was Chelsea playing, and he grinned and said that they were practising. I couldn't wait to get through the turnstile and find out what was behind that wall.

Inside the ground I was in heaven, seeing my heroes in the flesh. They seemed to have halos around them, the television and poster images coming to life in front of my eyes, but as well as watching the players I spent a lot of the game watching the end from where the singing came. Thousands of heads were packed in tight under the roof – swaying, swearing, chanting, clapping. It was the focal point of the ground and a hundred times more exciting than where we were standing. This was my first impression of the Shed, and this experience is probably very similar to that of thousands of others going to football for the first time, whatever club they support. I knew the Shed was where I wanted to be. The home end was passionate and out of control, the police moving in to grab boys and youths and chuck them out of the ground.

The '90s have seen the mass commercialisation of football, with a parade of media darlings spotting a good career move and suddenly swearing how much they love the game. They pretend they never went to football in the '70s and '80s because it was 'violent' and 'racist', when what they really mean is that they found it 'common'. They say football has never been so popular, but this is a lie. Everyone I grew up with was into football. It was part of our lives as teenagers, up there with music, drink, clothes and girls. There were over 44,000 people at that Southampton game, and attendances in the '70s were generally huge compared with those of today, while crowds in previous decades were higher still. What these media whores really mean is that there has never been so much money available, and they want their share.

The great terraces have been ripped down and business interests allowed to sanitise the game as it searches for a more wealthy audience, pushing out the kids and the less well-off, attempting to rewrite history. The atmosphere has been crushed and the passion blunted inside the stadiums, yet the spirit of each club continues outside, in the pubs and on the streets. Each club has its own flavour, and this is created by the supporters, who last a lot longer than the players, managers and chairmen. For many males, a reputation as good fighters matters more than the on-field performances, a question of pride and identity.

From the school playground to the football terraces, boys want to rebel. For a nine-year-old, the thought of going in the Shed was the ultimate. As I got older and interested in music and style, the whole thing fitted together as skinheads faded and boot boys took over, then shifted again as punk and 2 Tone arrived. In the mid '70s a good pair of Dr Martens was more important than a club shirt. While I liked the football, it was the whole culture that made me spend a good proportion of my money going to matches, travelling up and down the country, having a drink and a laugh. If there had been no crowd, no Shed, I probably wouldn't have bothered. Thousands felt the same way.

Going to Chelsea as a teenager was all about going in the Shed, but then it was about going up the North Stand and in Gate 13, meeting up at Euston or wherever to travel north on grim British Rail trains to grim cities where the locals wanted to batter the 'cockney bastards' and the police were just as friendly, about the pubs and clubs and drink, the endless stories and rumours, buzzing on the excitement as we ran up and down city streets. It has been the same for hundreds of thousands of British boys/youths/men through the years, right across the land.

There has always been an edge to football, the natural result of the passion that makes it special. It was, and is, a way of life, something outsiders can never understand, the media preferring inaccurate and scandalous stories written from the safety of plush offices by journalists with no idea of the reality. This book goes a long way to setting the record straight, capturing the mood of what a lot of people describe as the most exciting days of their lives. It would be stupid to say there wasn't some serious violence along with the pitch invasions and punch-ups, but this is often overplayed by outsiders, while for most of those who were actually there, the great days of the '70s and '80s are remembered just as much for the comradeship and humour.

Football-related violence is nothing new. The father of a family friend, now dead, once told me how as a young man before the war he used to follow West Ham, how when they went down to Millwall the fighting started in the morning, continued through the game and then went on late into the night. Since the '60s, though, the amount of trouble has greatly increased, a combination of emerging youth cults and more sensationalist media reporting – among other factors. The media have played their part, and hypocritical journalists will no doubt try and dismiss *Hoolifan* as a glorification of violence. It is nothing of the sort. It doesn't justify or condemn, just tells the truth. This is what social history should be like:

an honest look at an area of our culture that is consistently misreported. *Hoolifan* captures the feel of something that has affected hundreds of thousands of males and talks about some famous London characters who, without this book, might never have been recorded in print – 'the most famous unfamous names in London', as Martin Knight likes to call them.

The very title of this book questions the term 'hooligan'. To me, a hooligan is a kid who sprays subways and smashes up phone boxes, but the Establishment has adopted it as a catch-phrase to describe many different sorts of people. The old chestnut that a 'true fan' never swears or fights at football, just sits there like a moron in a replica shirt, politely clapping the opposition as he stuffs a rip-off burger down his throat, is ridiculous, and this book isn't afraid to stand up and say so.

As with the better crime books, *Hoolifan* gives an insight into areas of our society that would otherwise never be recorded in print. The history of the everyday man and woman is generally passed on in conversation, an oral tradition that eventually sees the stories die out. When it is written down, it is normally by an outsider, an academic with no personal experience or real understanding of the subject, writing from the outside looking in. This book is the authentic item.

One of the great strengths of *Hoolifan* is that it is written by people who know what they are talking about and who have been honest in what they say, mixing the good with the bad. Another is that they are able to write. Martin Knight was a follower of Eccles in the '70s and was able to observe events at close hand before getting married and stepping back from the scene. Martin King, meanwhile, is a well-known face at Chelsea and has been in evidence for the last thirty years. He is what some people would describe as a 'top boy'. Tough, honest and funny, this book is essential reading – a terrace-culture classic.

ONE

Daddy's Boy

'Come on, boy, hurry up or we'll be late. Come on!'

'All right, I'm coming. I'm just putting me boots on.'

It is a cold, very cold, winter's Saturday and my dad is about to take me to my first ever football match. We're off to see the great Spurs double-winning side of the early '60s. I am going to see people like Danny Blanchflower, Dave Mackay and John White in real life. In real life! I can't believe it.

'Wrap yerself up, boy,' says Mum as she fusses over my scarf and coat buttons. 'Look after him, Fred. Don't let him out of your sight.'

'He's all right,' smiles Dad as he ruffles my hair. Mum nods as she looks me up and down, a cigarette clenched between her lips but not dropping the three inches of ash which is precariously balanced on the end.

So off we go to White Hart Lane to see Tottenham Hotspur play the less glamorous Nottingham Forest. But I don't mind; I'm six years old and can barely contain my excitement. The long walk from our house in Mitcham, Surrey, to Colliers Wood Underground station seems to take forever. We take the tube to Manor House and from there it's another long trek to the ground; don't forget there is no Victoria Line yet. Finally we reach the stadium and the atmosphere hits me like I have just run smack bang into a wall.

Dad grips my gloved hand. 'Hold tight, boy. If I lose you yer muvver will kill me.'

I can't take it all in. I'm outside a real football stadium.

People are rushing and scurrying around in every direction. My nostrils are assaulted by the distinctive smell of hot dogs cooking on the roadside, and men in white coats are shouting their wares. Flogging programmes, rosettes, scarves, badges and photos of the Tottenham heroes. Rushing men dressed in heavy, dark overcoats with shirts and ties underneath bustle past, looking down at the ground – but they know instinctively where they are going. Many are wearing flat caps so familiar from old Pathé News clips of past FA Cup finals; most are puffing on fags.

It looks like there is going to be a full house, but at last we're inside after being pushed and shoved around for what seemed an age. Time is moving on and we hurry up the steep steps to the terrace, and the noise explodes. The teams run out on to the pitch and nearly fifty thousand men go wild. They shake wooden rattles around their heads as if about to launch a boomerang; the less energetic flourish their dark blue and white scarves. I can remember the crackling noise that those thousands of rattles made in the cold afternoon air; it is a sound that no one under the age of thirty could ever have heard.

I don't really follow the game, although there is plenty of action, the match finishing 4–1 to Spurs. I am transfixed by the atmosphere and the crowd. Grown men jump up and down like children when the goals go in, men older than Dad shout and swear and no one tells them off. This is party time, big time, and I want it all the time.

At the end of the game we head for the exits and squeeze out on to the Seven Sisters Road, but the long walk back to Manor House doesn't seem to take so long as I savour the day.

'Did you enjoy that, boy?' smiles Dad as he looks down sideways at me.

'Yeah, brilliant Dad. I can't wait to tell the kids at school and can't wait to be Danny Blanchflower in the playground! Will you take me again, Dad?' I say, hurrying to keep up with his grown-up steps.

'We'll see,' he replies, and he pats me on the head.

'Thanks for taking me, Dad.'

I look up again and he's smiling.

We did go to football again about a month or so later. This time Dad took me to Craven Cottage to see Fulham and Sunderland play. Fulham were no Tottenham but they had a big star in Johnny Haynes and the ground was packed. The atmosphere was unlike White Hart Lane; it was still exciting and I loved it, but the crowd had a different flavour. In later life I would muse on how crowds of different clubs could have their own individual character, but they clearly did. That Fulham crowd was sort of laid-back, enjoying themselves but not so intense about the outcome. Perhaps that's why I don't remember the score.

The old man didn't only take me to football. We also saw speedway, boxing, wrestling and cricket. You name it, we watched it. I think it gave him pleasure, not just spectating but the fact it gave me such a buzz. I'd catch him sneaking a look at my face as I drank in the atmosphere at these events. My older brother, Alan, was not at all interested in sport of any description, so it was me who travelled London and beyond with Dad to watch anyone play. Before I was ten I had visited football grounds as far apart as Portsmouth and Ipswich, and we would catch as many different teams as we could when they visited London. We didn't care whether it was First Division or Southern League: if it was a football match, we were there. Saturday was football day, with fish and chips and Tizer for dinner in the evening.

One weekend we visited Stamford Bridge, home of Chelsea Football Club. They were entertaining Manchester United, possibly the most famous club in the world and certainly the one with the biggest following in England. Sixty thousand were expected and it was set to be a great game, with both clubs doing well in the league. A couple of years or more had passed since my Tottenham debut and I knew a lot more about the game. Football was on fire. England had won the World Cup and the First Division sported an array of superstars. Manchester United offered up Bobby Charlton, George Best and Denis Law, whilst Chelsea, who hadn't yet entered their glamour and champagne phase, boasted the likes of Tony Hateley, Bobby Tambling and Terry Venables.

Dad and I arrived at Fulham Broadway via Wimbledon on the District Line. The tube was packed and we swung backwards and forwards with the rhythm of the train as it rattled over the Thames. Dad clutched one of those things that hang out of the ceiling and I just bounced off the people around me. I was too old now for holding the old man's hand. The train pulled in and the doors squeaked open. As if acting on a command, the passengers made a mad rush for the stairs leading out on to the Fulham Road. Minutes before they had been having quiet, sensible conversations with one another, yet now they were running and leaping up the stairs as if they had fireworks up their arses. As at Spurs I was being pushed, pulled, squashed and squeezed, but then I was out in the fresh air at the entrance of Fulham Broadway station. The crowd started to walk now. Some walked straight across the road towards the White Hart, others turned right, but the majority, including us, turned left and pushed our way up the Fulham Road towards the ground.

'Programmes, programmes, get yer match programmes!' was the first cry I heard.

'Hot dogs, hot dogs!'

'Roasted chestnuts, 6d a bag!'

'Wear ya colours, get ya Chelsea scarves here!' shouted the man outside the North Stand who was offering woollen scarves in the colours of both teams to all who passed him. It was mad. It was still an hour before kick-off but there was a sea of people washing all over the area. This seemed like a cup final to me. I noticed police horses, lots of them. I hadn't spotted any at Spurs, Fulham or the other grounds we had visited. The police on foot looked troubled as they tried to marshal us into queues. We obliged, and after half an hour of pushing and shoving I was at the turnstile.

'Stop pushing! There are kids here, for fuck's sake!' shouted one angry dad.

'Take yer time, you'll all get in,' said the old boy clicking the turnstile as he dropped another bob into his pocket.

After entering the ground, I blinked in the sunlight and looked up at the steps to the terrace. Whoever thought up turnstile entrances at football grounds has a lot to answer for. How the fuck they get thousands of bodies through a three-foot gap with no orderly queuing system is beyond me. After a hundred years of soccer stadiums, still no one has found a better and safer alternative. It is enough to make the most placid spectator bad-tempered by the time he gains entry.

We took our positions just below the Bovril tea bar. I could see the whole of the ground and it made the other ones I had visited look almost poky. It was an afternoon game but the floodlights were on, adding to the allure. Sixty-six thousand people stood shoulder to shoulder, and at least half of them were wearing the red and white colours of Manchester United. The teams trotted out of the tunnel and on to the pitch to an almighty roar, and necks craned across the ground. Dad hoisted me on to his shoulders; I was level with thousands of wooden rattles being shaken furiously. There was no singing, just men shouting and the clattering of the rattles.

The game finished in a draw. Everyone was happy. We made the short walk back to the underground but had to queue for about an hour just to cram on to a homeward-bound train. I had ample opportunity to study my surroundings. The pubs teeming with supporters of both teams. The flats and the terraced streets running off the Fulham Road. The balcony where a bunch of rough-looking teenagers leaned against the railings, chewing gum and eyeing the queuing masses. Those pubs, that balcony and the terraced backstreets were to figure time and time again for me in the coming years.

Back at home, Mum was watching TV. She got up and made us hot drinks. I drank mine and, unusually for me, went voluntarily to bed. I was worn out by all that walking, queuing and excitement. I lay there with the images of the floodlights, the players from Charles Buchan's *Football Monthly* who had come to life and the huge crowd swirling around my head. The noise was still with me, especially the rattles, and the smell of cigarette smoke lingered on in my nostrils. The trains were smoky and so was the ground. Everyone seemed to be lit up, mainly with fags but there were plenty of pipes too. The combined smoke hung over the ground and the surrounding area. I can remember the smell; it is a lost smell. Dad walked into the room. I was very lucky to have as a dad a football nut who enjoyed taking his son out at every opportunity. I was never embarrassed to be seen with him, even as I got older. He was my dad and my best mate.

'Dad,' I asked, 'would you make me one of those rattles?'

'Sure, boy, what colour? Red and white or blue and white?'

I thought about it for a few seconds. United were exciting but they would only be in London a few times a year. Chelsea would be here every other week. It could have easily been Spurs or Dad's team, Fulham, but I had made my mind up.

'Blue and white, Dad. I'm going to support Chelsea from now on.'

TWO

Saturday Morning Pictures

There goes the final whistle. Spurs have won the 1967 FA Cup final 2–1. The Chelsea players plod up the stairs at Wembley to receive their runners-up medals; they look gutted. But not half as gutted as me. I am at home with Mum and Dad, chairs pulled up close to the telly on this black and white Saturday in May. 'Gutted' is a good word; that's how I really feel, my stomach churning away but my insides empty as well. I get up.

'I'm off out,' I announce.

If I hang around I think I might cry. I swallow hard and walk out into the street. It's not going to be any better out here. I'm bound to get tons of stick off the other kids, many of whom support Manchester United, Liverpool, Leeds, Nottingham Forest and even Spurs. When I say 'support', I mean 'support' only as in the way my Dad 'supports' the British Leyland workers when they go on strike – he supports them but he does fuck all about it. These kids don't go; they don't follow. They've got no right to dig me out. Give them a map of Britain and they'd be hard-pressed to pick out any of the cities these teams come from. Anyway, I want to face them now – less grief at school on Monday, I figure. I can front it out. I'm twelve years old and proud to be a Chelsea fan. They know I go regular with the old man. They only see it on *Match of the Day* on a Saturday night and *Star Soccer* on a Sunday afternoon, and then they're in the comfortable surroundings of their own homes with their rented black and white DER tellies crackling away in the corner.

At first there aren't many out in the street. *Dr Who* must be on. A lot of the boys like that, but I think it's shit. Soon, though, a group of scruffy children appear in the road.

'Spurs were lucky,' I say, getting my attack in first. 'Anyway, I'm not that bothered.'

'That's shit,' pipes up one of the many Ballard brothers. 'Chelsea played shit and we can tell by your face you are bothered.'

There are a few around me now, laughing and goading. One kid is singing '2–1, 2–1, 2–1' from behind one of the bigger Ballards.

'Least we got to the final,' I shrug, still trying to act nonchalant.

'Yeah, but yer lost,' spits the youngest and fattest of the Ballard clan.

'Shut yer mouth, Arbuckle, you little piglet,' I retort, feeling the blood rushing up to my face. And now they are all singing '2–1, 2–1, 2–1'. I kick a football straight at them and run back to the house. Wait till one of their teams loses. I'll show them. I'll make their lives hell. But they are not real fans; they won't really care.

The next time we got to meet Tottenham Hotspur was at White Hart Lane the following season. I was looking forward to watching Chelsea's revenge but was horrified when Dad told me he couldn't take me because he had to do some overtime at work. He knew I was upset and promised he'd be off for the next home game.

'Dad, can I go with some of the older boys from school?' I pleaded. These boys were only around fourteen and fifteen years old; Dad and I had seen them at Stamford Bridge now and then and said hello. But to me they were as adult as my dad.

'I'll speak to your mum. If she says yes, you can go.'

I worked on her all week, I was that desperate. I washed up the dishes, ran to the corner shop for her fags, made cups of tea and even took the dog out. By the morning of the game she still hadn't committed herself. She was enjoying the new me and milking every minute of it.

'Who are you thinking of going to this game with, boy?' she eventually asked casually.

'What game, Mum?' I said, frantically playing for time as I assembled in my head some names of boys my mum would deem to come from good families. Responsible boys with paper rounds I would be safe with.

'The game today, who are you thinking of going with?'

I reeled off a list of names, mixing in some of the real people I was tagging along with so it wasn't a complete lie.

'All right,' she smiled. 'That's enough grovelling for one week. You can go, but keep clear of trouble. Wrap yerself up and come straight home.'

Before the words had passed the tip of her cigarette, I was up the stairs. I collected a few bits and pieces. I stopped and looked at the blue and white rattle Dad had made me, spoilt brat that I was, but didn't pick it up. I didn't think the older boys would like it. I slid down the stairs.

'See ya,' I yelled as the door crashed shut behind me. Coming up the front path was Alan, my older brother. His hair was unkempt and he looked like he'd slept the night in a hedge. Probably had. He'd been out all night on the piss. He asked where I was rushing off to. I told him and he pressed a pound note into my eager hand. He staggered on into the house. He always gave me money when he'd had a drink.

'Thanks, Al, you're the best brother in the world.'

'I know,' he said.

It was only 10.30 a.m. but I knocked for the others and the three of us set off from Mitcham Fairgreen for a bus to Tooting Broadway and then a train to Liverpool Street and from there a dirty green British Rail train to White Hart Lane. The north London-bound train seemed very empty.

'Not a very good turnout, is it Jeff?' I observed.

'It's early yet,' replied Jeff with the air of a seasoned football fan. 'There are four hours to go to kick-off. I'm sure we'll bump into some Chelsea around the ground.'

'I hope so,' I muttered, nervously fingering my blue and white woollen scarf which was knotted tightly around my neck like some oversized tie. As I surveyed the carriage, with its customary debris of fag ends, the previous night's piss and footprinted pages of the *Daily Sketch* rolling around, I began to feel apprehensive about the adventure that lay ahead. Four hours until kick-off!

'What'll we do when we get there?' I asked.

'Well, we can't go in the pub cos you're here.'

Cheeky bastards. They couldn't get in a pub whether I was with them or not.

'Right, here we are. Let's go!' shouted Jeff, jumping from the slowing train as it squealed into White Hart Lane station. I was soon to learn that it was compulsory for young football fans to disembark from trains in this fashion. And last one out has to slam the door. Train doors were crashing up and down the length of the platform but besides this there was no noise. No chanting fans. No police. No one. Just a few Saturday shoppers leisurely going about their business. We rushed past the ticket collector and he made no attempt to ask to see our tickets. Normal BR procedures were abandoned on Saturday afternoons. Down the stairs and into the street, still no fans. We were early. Not even the hot-dog sellers were here yet to get a prime pitch.

'Wait here, Martin,' Jeff tells me as he and Dave nip into a shop to buy some fags.

Perhaps they think the shopkeeper won't serve them if he sees me. I peer up and down the road for signs of life. Where is the crowd and the electric atmosphere I'm used to when Dad and I go to games? What do we do for the next three hours? Better get a programme, I think, that'll while away some time. Suddenly I hear a rumbling noise. I feel it as well. The ground beneath my feet is vibrating – and then the rumbling turns into a loud roar. I look across the road and coming out of the Paxton Road side of the ground is a mob of Spurs fans. It seems like there are thousands of them, charging towards the spot where I happen to be standing. Instinct takes over and I burst into the shop.

'Don't go out there yet,' I splutter. 'There's thousands of them.' I try to catch my breath.

'Who?' they ask in unison.

'Spurs fans. There's thousands of them.'

We look wide-eyed out of the shop window as this herd of buffalo in Spurs colours gallops past, leaving clouds of dust in its wake. They are screaming and their eyes are popping out of their heads. Some are smiling and laughing. Standing there in the shop, transfixed by the spectacle taking place in front of us, it reminds me of Saturday morning pictures at the cinema, watching a wildlife film on a wide-screen. They pour around the corner and head towards the station we have just arrived at.

'Look at their mob,' sighs Jeff, his mouth wide open. Then, as the reality of the situation dawns on him, he orders, 'Quick, put yer scarves away, and if anyone asks who you support, tell 'em Spurs.'

We brace ourselves to walk back out on to the street. We're shitting it, but the mob has passed and we look a bit suspect just standing in a shop. Jeff opens the door cautiously and promptly shuts it again. The same mob are heading straight back towards us. This time they are running twice as fast and the look on their faces is different. It is the look of fear.

We return to our cinema seats and watch the next instalment. The shopkeeper has joined us now – concerned about his window going in, no doubt. The Spurs fans are running for their lives. On the way up they were in a tight, compact group; now they are scattered across the whole road, falling over one another in their haste, running into and over cars, jumping fences and darting down alleys and side roads. Some stop and walk in a different direction, hoping they can blend in with shoppers and pedestrians. The bulk of them, though, disappear back down the Paxton Road from where they had come.

'Chel-SEA, Chel-SEA, Chel-SEA, Chel-SEA!' We can hear the chant but we can't see the fans. They sing 'Chelsea' at the Bridge but in a jolly, friendly way. This is like a war cry. It's threatening. The Spurs mob has almost evaporated. One big lad shouts, 'Stand, stand,' but no one is. I don't think he really means it. He's walking backwards. Now he's running. I suppose he'll tell them all in the pub how he tried to hold it together. Suddenly the Chelsea gang are all around the shop. The chase is over and they're all looking pleased with themselves. They pat each other on the shoulders, which are heaving up and down as they recapture their breath. Jeff and Dave take their scarves out and put them back around their necks. I do the same and we amble out of the shop and stand among them.

'Fucking Tottenham scumbags,' says one.

'What's up with them fucking Yids? They never stand,' chips in another.

Later I was to learn that Spurs fans were called Yids or Yiddos on account of the team's large Jewish following. They were older than me, these boys, and older than Jeff and Dave, but not by much. I reckon the average age was sixteen or seventeen. One boy looked like a man. He had long, black sideboards. His hands were thrust in his pockets and he was speaking; I couldn't hear what he was saying but a lot of the boys crowded around him and were hanging on his every word. He had an air about him. He was the focus. What struck me more than anything, though, were the clothes everyone wore. They looked smart. They looked the part. I felt out of place in my monkey jacket and Tesco jeans. 'Tesco tearaways' someone at home had called them when showing me his new Levi jeans, after he had sat in the bath all day with them on to get that important washed-out look. Only a couple of years back my monkey jacket – or World Cup jacket, as they were also called – had been my pride and joy. They had come out after the World Cup when the victorious England team had worn them at the training ground. They were blue anorak-type things with red and white cuffs and collar. These guys wouldn't be seen dead in one, I knew straight away. Meanwhile, Jeff and Dave continued chatting with some of them.

'What happened?' enquired Jeff, speaking to an older boy called Martin.

'We come off the train and out on to the road and there's this mob of Yids coming round the corner. There's about five hundred of us and they see us and 'ave it on their toes. Not a punch thrown.'

'Where d'yer get yer trousers?' I interrupted.

Martin looked down at me with a puzzled look on his face.

'Who's this apprentice wanker examining my wardrobe?' he was thinking. Dave and Jeff stared at me pointedly, wishing I wasn't there.

'At the army surplus store up the Elephant.'

'What are they called?' I asked, noticing that loads of the Chelsea boys were wearing them.

'Jungle greens.'

'How much?'

'Two quid.'

'Did you get yer boots there as well?'

'Yeah, cherry red commando boots – four quid. Your little mate's a nosy fucker, ain't he Jeff?' Martin laughed.

'He's all right,' Jeff replied. 'If it wasn't for him we'd have been mincemeat just now when the Spurs came past.'

Jeff said we should stay with this lot and we swaggered up the road with them. I was fascinated and bombarded Jeff with questions. They came from Tooting Junction, Battersea, Stockwell and Fulham, he explained.

'Who's the bloke with the sideboards?'

'They call him Eccles.'

'Is he the sort of leader?'

'Yeah, sort of.'

'How old is he?'

'About eighteen,' said Jeff, getting a bit impatient now.

'How did he become leader?' I asked. I thought of when we played football down the park; we picked two captains and they then picked their teams alternately from a line-up.

'I don't fucking know. Now shut up and keep up with this lot.'

I shut up but made a mental note to ask Jeff where the shop 'Up the Elephant' was.

Into the ground we go, behind the goal where the Spurs fans are already gathered. This part of the ground is called the Park Lane and it is where the home supporters always congregate. It is Tottenham's Shed. We follow the Chelsea supporters across the terrace. I am feeling secure in the middle of the mob from outside, despite the scared faces I witnessed earlier. I don't really understand what is happening. We are heading towards the Spurs fans, ducking under safety barriers and pushing through the crowd. These people we push through could be Chelsea fans or they could be Tottenham fans, but they look straight ahead and take a small step forwards or backwards to let us pass. That look says quite clearly, 'I am not part of this. I am looking ahead. I am here to watch football.' Now we reach a double barrier running from the top of the terrace to the bottom. In the gap stands a line of policemen, the first I have seen all day.

'Wait here,' shouts the bloke they call Eccles. 'When we are all together, we'll give it a push.'

The Spurs fans, however, suss it and make a push towards us. Of course, they're not going anywhere with the metal barrier and the police line holding them back. The policemen ride the surge and bounce the Tottenham boys back; they laugh and wink to one another. They don't seem cross and it looks like they're enjoying their crucial role. But Chelsea are still coming in and the end is getting fuller and fuller. I can see them moving towards us – a moving snake of young men in an end of stationary people.

Both sets of fans are surging now and I am joining in by pushing my shoulder up against the lower back of the big bloke in front. The teams come on to the pitch and the fans vie to make the most noise. The atmosphere is charged. Not like when I came here for my first game and not like any other match I have been to since. The atmosphere is charged with sheer hate. Everyone around me is spitting out insults, eyes are bulging, blue veins protrude from foreheads and fists are being waved wildly across the terrace. But I'm not scared. I'm with Chelsea, and hadn't they already chased the Tottenham boys away? I am more intrigued. Did they really feel this strongly? Everyone was quite happy outside. And why? Okay, Tottenham had beaten us in the FA Cup final. But they hadn't cheated. That's football, isn't it? And Jimmy Robertson's goal was a real cracker in anyone's book!

But now there are coins and bottles being lobbed by both sides, and the boys around me are coughing up phlegm and spitting across at the Tottenham. The Spurs fans are shifting to the front as the crowd bears down from the top. Chelsea are in there too, at the top of the terrace. I can see the same fear on faces that I had seen from the shop. The younger Spurs fans are panicking now and climbing over the small wall at the bottom of the terrace, jumping on to the safety of the pitch. Chelsea are still pouring down, punching and kicking their way through. The kids are getting tangled up in the goal nets as they try and run whilst keeping one eye on the developing chaos on the terrace.

The first group I am with sense that control is slipping away from the police as they, too, are watching the top of the terrace. They start to duck under the barrier and dash across the no-man's land, into the Spurs fans. I follow. The police grab a few of us and throw us back but the dam has burst. There is nowhere to go for the Spurs fans. I can't see a lot but know I am in the middle of a riot. I can tell by the faces near to me that order has gone. Some people are revelling in the anarchy but others are scared. Really scared. Police reinforcements are arriving and somehow they manage to throw a cordon around the now heavily outnumbered Tottenham supporters. The smiles have disappeared from the faces of the Old Bill. They are angry now. Their fun day out on overtime has been ruined and they sense a situation that could turn very nasty.

The half-time whistle goes and it seems to have a calming effect on proceedings. The fighting subsides. The police regain their composure and start shoving Chelsea fans over or under the barrier. Boys are getting ejected and arrested all around me and this quietens everyone down. The second half passes almost without incident; the occasional bottle or coin is thrown and there are a few surges, but nothing like the performance I had seen in the first forty-five minutes.

There I was, twelve years old, and I had witnessed my first incidence of football violence. Blokes around me were sporting black eyes and bloody noses but none seemed really hurt. I'm not sure how they got them because I didn't actually see anyone close to me get punched or kicked. But my head had been down and I had been surrounded all the time by the bigger lads. I had been in a riot but I had been below sea-level.

Spurs fans had been damaged more, I guessed – at least, their egos had. There was no doubt that Chelsea fans had battered and humiliated them in their own end.

We all crammed into the train back to Liverpool Street. Everyone was talking excitedly about what had gone on and how Chelsea had given Spurs a severe kicking.

'That's for last season at Wembley,' declared one big skinhead. Funny, I thought, that was the first time I had heard football mentioned all day.

Another big lump of a teenager was stretched out above us in the luggage rack, his huge denim-clad arse stretching the netting to its limits.

'Next week we've got Man United, so let's hope everyone turns up to give them red bastards a dose of what we've just given the Yids.'

With that everyone cheered and a chorus of 'Chelsea, Chelsea, Chelsea!' broke out up and down the train.

As the train pulled back into Liverpool Street, the doors were flying open the minute the driver nosed the first carriage level with the platform. Kids were jumping off, landing on the ground and running alongside the moving train, desperately trying to slow down but their little legs going like piston rods doing a hundred miles an hour. Jeff was one of the first off and was encouraging me to jump. I felt like John Mills in one of those old British films we watched on a Sunday afternoon, flying jacket on, ready to parachute out of a Second World War fighter plane.

'Jump, you wanker, jump!'

'Fuck off,' I replied, but I was shoved from behind and my body was in mid-air. My feet hit the platform and my legs went like the clappers to keep my body upright. I had done it. Only some time later did I cotton on that only the most dickhead football fans disembarked from trains in this way.

Back on the Northern Line, it was down to just the three of us again and we were gently coming down off the day's high. We got off at Colliers Wood and then had the familiar walk back to Mitcham, via George's Fish Bar at Poole's Corner, where we all bought saveloy and chips. Finally I split with the others and strolled down the road to my house. Dad walked towards me; he was off down the chippy for his and Mum's supper.

'Howdit go, boy?'

'Great,' I beamed.

'What was the score?' Dad asked, although I think he knew.

I looked at him blankly. I blinked. I looked down at the pavement. Found a bit of saveloy in between my teeth and made a big thing about retrieving it. I didn't know the score. I had no idea. I still don't.

THREE

Football and Fashion

'Any trouble there yesterday?' Dad asked, fixing his eye on me.

'Didn't see any,' I shrugged.

It was Sunday morning and Dad had his usual selection of Sunday tabloids spread across his chair. It was normal practice for him to read the papers from the back to the front, sports pages first. Mum busied herself in the kitchen and the first waves of Sunday roast aromas were beginning to waft into the sitting-room. On the floor, one headline screamed, 'WHAT IS FOOTBALL COMING TO?' It was accompanied by some pictures of the Tottenham crowd disturbances.

'Want locking up, the lot of them, bloody hooligans,' he snorted. 'You were there, boy, and you never saw any of it?'

'That's right, Dad. I never saw none of that what the papers are saying.'

'Well,' he continued, 'if the police don't get a grip on this sort of thing and sort these thugs out, things will get out of hand.'

How right he was. He was just an ordinary football fan. He was no politician or expert from university, but that Sunday afternoon in 1968 he could see the graffiti on the wall. Now, thirty years on, the so-called best brains in Britain struggle to find a solution. Perhaps if the powers that were had consulted ordinary working-class football fans back in the days when it all kicked off, they could have nipped it in the bud. But no, it was left to arseholes who had gone to schools where football was considered too 'common' a game for them to play.

There were forty-four arrests at the White Hart Lane game, thirty-six juveniles and eight adults. Charges included insulting behaviour, obstructing the police and carrying offensive weapons. According to the papers, these included a meat hook, a metal cosh, weighted sand bags (how did they get them in?), bagged coins, leather straps, paint sprays and various hammers. Most of those forty-four drew paltry ten-pound fines. I reckon that if the courts had started dishing out stiff sentences then, impressionable youngsters like myself would have been less likely to cause trouble and associate themselves with the troublemakers. End of story, methinks. Instead they allowed a whole culture to grow, a culture that would permeate young working-class society across Britain and, later, Europe.

The following Saturday Chelsea were playing host to the great Manchester United team, and at 7.30 sharp Jeff, Colin and Tony were knocking on my front door.

'You're fucking joking! Him up at this time?' I heard Mum say as I lay in bed. 'What d'you want him for at this bleedin' hour?'

'We're going up the Elephant to buy some of those jungle green trousers all the boys had on at Tottenham last week,' explained Jeff.

'Wot, this early?' I yawned, now standing beside Mum.

'You said come round early,' piped up Tony, 'so get yerself ready and let's go.'

I had a quick cat's lick, as Dad would call it; this entailed splashing as little water on my face as possible. None on my ears or neck. This was the morning wash according to the gospel of soap-dodgers.

Mum was following me from room to room, the first fag of the day burning away in her mouth.

'How comes you're off so early? Ain't you going to football with your Dad later?'

I told her about the army trousers called jungle greens we had seen.

'What are fucking jungle greens when they're at home?' she said. 'How you gonna pay for them, boy?'

'I was hoping you was going to lend me the money.'

I smiled as charmingly as I could.

'Lend you the money! What d'you think – we're made of money?' She was shouting now. 'Hold up, I'll just pop into the back garden and pick some off the fucking money tree, shall I?'

Mornings were not Mum's best time. I hung my head a little and told the boys they should go without me and perhaps I'd see them later. Embarrassed by my mum's outburst, they scurried back out of the front door.

'Thanks a lot for showing me up, Mum.'

'Any time, boy,' she replied sarcastically.

Just then the old man let himself in. He asked why I wasn't with my mates whom he had just seen leaving the house. I told him about the trousers, the Elephant and that Mum had said there was no money. Before he could think about it, I asked if I could borrow two quid off him for the trousers and another quid for the Man U game. He fished in his pocket and gave me three crisp, green pound notes and a bit of shrapnel.

'I want it back, mind,' he said, more for Mum's benefit, I reckon, knowing that I had no income to pay him back with. 'Keep out of trouble,' he added. 'You know what happened last week.'

'Of course, Dad.'

I glanced at Mum, who was standing, arms folded, with her 'I give up, you spoilt little bastard' look on her face, and I scarpered before anyone could change their mind. I ran like the clappers and caught up my pals at Colliers Wood tube station.

'You got the money, then?' assumed Tony.

'Yeah, yeah. Just had to work on the old lady a bit,' I lied, not wanting to admit that it was Dad who had coughed up in the end.

As we sat on the train, I looked up at the tube map and counted the stops to Elephant and Castle, our destination. It was not many stops on the black line, but it could have been another country when we were kids. Colin started to talk about Millwall and how they were playing at home and lots of their fans came from the Elephant and surrounding areas.

'I hope we don't bump into any,' he expanded. 'They're all six-foot-six-inch dockers, about forty years old, and they hate Chelsea.'

For a second or two I had a mental image of hordes of young Arthur Mullards with fists like sledgehammers, wearing donkey jackets and prowling around south London. Common sense prevailed, though; grown men were hardly likely to be hanging around at 8.30 on a Saturday morning to bash three Chelsea fans half their size and barely in their teens. I didn't say anything, though, not wanting to burst the bubble of excitement.

We found the army surplus store and there in the window were the famous jungle greens with the two-pound price tag. Anyone would have thought we'd struck gold. I think we honestly believed this was the only place in the world where these prized items were available. We rushed into the shop, bought our respective sizes and quickly returned home, not wishing to encounter any early-rising dockers. After having the legs turned up and sewn to the required length, we met up again at Colin's house to set off for the United game. We all felt so good in our new trousers. It was like we had acquired membership of some special society. Colin's dad, though, thought it was hilarious and couldn't stop laughing at us. He said we looked like a platoon of midget army cadets about to go out on manoeuvres.

At the Bridge I stopped to buy a programme, which was full of the trouble at Tottenham the previous week. There were two pages with action pictures and the now familiar headline – 'WHAT IS FOOTBALL COMING TO?' Everyone had the little programme open at these pages and the pictures were the main subject of pre-match conversation. No one seemed ashamed or denounced the trouble in any way; in fact, it was the source of great pride in the Shed that day. The club had seen fit to write about the supporters. We had been officially recognised. Of the four of us at today's game, only myself and Jeff had been at White Hart Lane, and we let Tony and Colin and anyone else within earshot know what they had missed. Our account was suitably embellished, Jeff and I almost believing the exaggerated version of events that we were recounting. We described tactical manoeuvres, acts of extreme bravery, charges led by General Eccles and Field-Marshal Greenaway, bloodshed and glorious victory – and everyone else was doing the same. Soccer violence folklore was being created that afternoon in 1968 on the steps of the Shed.

I hadn't even seen Greenaway at Tottenham and wouldn't come across him till some time later, but he was a much-talked-about figure at Chelsea even then. Apparently he had been a mascot during Chelsea's only ever championship-winning season of 1955. He introduced the 'Zigger Zagger' chant to London and had made it his own, and he and the Webb brothers are often credited with getting the Shed going in the mid to late '60s. A legend grew up around him. His face appears to bear the scars and dents of a battering or three; sometimes it is said he was thrown through a plate-glass window in Manchester. Other stories tell of a vicious beating outside the Ifield pub, again by United fans. But in all my time I never saw him organising or indulging in violence of any kind. He loved Chelsea and he was always there. He got the boys going and he got them behind the team. He was a cheerleader and the hordes loved him, and he loved them. By the 1980s he was a mascot, again lauded by the fans as he got them singing 'One Man Went to Mow' up and down the country.

It was only 1.30 and the ground was packed, mainly with Manchester fans. It was not at this game, however, that I first saw United fans in action; it was at another London ground some time later. United had a phenomenal support in the 1960s and 1970s, both at home and away. Even in south London, in those days, every other kid followed them. Many of the kids from Mitcham supported Man U as their first club and Chelsea as their second, and I would sometimes travel with the Tooting and Mitcham Man United lot when their team was in London. Usually there did not seem to be any trouble – the sheer numbers that United brought just seemed to swamp whoever they were playing. One year, though, I went with Tony and some local kids to Highbury, where the Arsenal were entertaining their Old Trafford rivals. We had arrived in north London around noon and as soon as the turnstiles opened we entered the North Bank, Arsenal's famous end. We climbed the steps and looked down to see swarm upon swarm of United fans streaming in. Half an hour later, Man U had almost filled the centre of the North Bank. 'Arsenal, where are you?' they sang confidently.

'I couldn't see Chelsea taking this end as easily as we have,' boasted Johnny Hamilton, a United fan from Mitcham who was also a big-headed tosser. He was a few years older than us and delighted in picking on and bullying the younger ones amongst us. Some time later, though, we spied that Arsenal were beginning to mob up under the right-hand side of the cover of the North Bank. Then, from behind us, another local crew charged from the top, sending some of the United scampering into the steel toe-caps of the first mob we had spotted.

The numbers were still against the home side but more and more Arsenal were appearing from nowhere. They could see that the United lot, who relied on numbers to take over grounds, had no guts for a row. Johnny Hamilton and company were surrounded by Arsenal now. I looked around me and clocked the scared faces from Mitcham; they were shitting bricks, but Tony and I were not bothered. It wasn't that we were particularly brave, just that we were not United fans and did not feel like United fans, and our whole body language must have signified that. Anyway, there were enough real United fans from Manchester around for the Arsenal boys to humiliate. They stood out like erect penises in *Health and Efficiency* magazine. Loads of them were dressed like bikers, wearing either denim jackets or leather jackets with studs, and most had long, greasy hair.

In those days, northern and southern football fans really did dress differently. This was the skinhead era, remember. In the same way that the Chelsea boys impressed me on my visit to Spurs, threatening but smart in their Fred Perry shirts and jungle greens, it was at this Arsenal match that I first noticed the Ben Sherman shirt on mass display. The Arsenal fans were nearly all dressed in these checked shirts with button-down collars and a pleat running down the back topped with a pointless little hook. With their neatly cropped hair, two-tone tonic trousers and Ivy brogue shoes, I thought this lot looked the real business. United came out second best that day, not only on the pitch and on the terrace but also in the fashion stakes.

On the way home we ran into the dejected United fans on the tube. I smiled inwardly as I surveyed the Cockney Reds, as they were already calling themselves, quiet in the knowledge that they had been turned over on and off the field. I was especially enjoying the disappointment of the Mitcham would-be Mancunians. There were some Arsenal fans on the train, too, who came from down our way.

'I thought you lot never run,' laughed Steve Harris, an Arsenal boy from Mitcham who was greatly respected in our area. He was a hard nut but never put himself about. A gentleman among boys. The United lot just sat there and took the stick. I had known Steve Harris for years on account of the fact that our mums had worked together, and I felt safe enough to be able to join in his goading.

'Who was the big fella in the yellow checked Ben Sherman giving out all the orders to the Arsenal lot?' asked Dave Griffin, another Cockney Red among us.

'That's Johnny Hoy,' replied Steve. 'He's Arsenal's top boy. I noticed you lot kept well away from him. Today should teach you United boys that you can't just come to London grounds and take them over unless you've got the bollocks for a fight. And you lot ain't.'

Steve Harris was right, and so was my dad. He had drummed into me from an early age that bullies always get their comeuppance, as United had done that day. They were the biggest kid in the playground but they had come up against another kid who could have a ruck. It was well known that United had taken over West Ham's ground a couple of seasons before, wreaking havoc. I think it was this experience that made West Ham organise themselves a bit better, and to this day they hate United with a vengeance.

After the Arsenal rout, Manchester United's bubble seemed to burst in terms of taking over London grounds. The liberties they had taken in the late '60s at West Ham, Spurs, Arsenal and Chelsea were a thing of the past by the 1970s. As for

Arsenal, I've always had the greatest respect for their fans. At that time they had a fearsome mob and not many clubs dared go to Highbury and take the piss. Every season at Chelsea you could guarantee they'd put in an appearance in the Shed, and sometimes they took it. Chelsea fans like to think that only West Ham ever achieved this, but I can also recall the likes of Leeds, Forest and Everton clearing the Shed end at various times. Even Bristol City had a pop one year!

This was the time when it seemed the big northern clubs would visit the capital but London clubs rarely travelled north of Watford. You certainly wouldn't dream of a trip to Liverpool or Everton. The accepted wisdom was that if you were captured you'd be robbed of all your worldly belongings. We heard dozens of stories about London boys taking a pasting at the hands of scousers who then proceeded to strip them of their prized sheepskin coats, Levi sta-prests, Ben Shermans and boots, leaving them shivering on Merseyside in just their underpants. How true these stories were, I don't know. Perhaps a penny will drop in some former BR ticket collector's mind if he reads this, having puzzled for years about regularly having to quiz semi-naked teenagers about their lack of a ticket on Saturday evening Inter-Cities to London back in the late 1960s.

What was definitely true, though, was that the scousers were a million miles away from the image that the media liked to portray: all of them in the Kop swaying in the wind and tunefully singing songs by the Beatles and Gerry and the Pacemakers. A big thing was made of how they would sportingly clap the opposing goalkeeper when he ran to keep goal at the Kop end. If they could have got on to the pitch, not only would they have chored his little bag, gloves and cap, but he'd have been the first keeper to have played in just his pants! In reality, they were among the most violent supporters. They were striping people with Stanley knives on Merseyside when the rest of the world was labouring under the impression that they were designed for cutting carpet.

Not long after the Arsenal adventure, I purchased my first Ben Sherman, a red and blue checked number. I could have got a Brutus shirt earlier – these were a cheap imitation of the Sherman – but preferred to wait until I could afford the pukka item. What with the cropped hair, the jungles and my steel-toe-capped commando boots (which were three sizes too big but better than the Zutch monkey boots some of my mates had to settle for), I had the complete football fan's uniform.

I later changed my bovver boots (as they were universally known then) for a pair of perfect-fitting Dr Marten high-ups. These were bought from Holidge Brothers in Thornton Heath, who were making a pretty decent living from selling bovver boots to just about every aspiring skinhead in south London. It's hard to appreciate thirty years on just how widespread the skinhead movement was. Unlike youth cults that came along afterwards, like punk, most working-class teenagers followed skinhead fashion and immersed themselves in the culture to some degree. Skinheads liked football, reggae music and bank-holiday visits to the coast. Some inherited scooters from their older brothers who had been mods. Greasers were the natural enemy, as the rockers were to the mods, and hippies were for taking the piss out of. Football violence didn't spawn skinheads, neither did skinheads invent soccer hooliganism, but the two phenomena came to national prominence together as the 1960s became the 1970s and have been inseparable in the minds of most people ever since.

Trouble at football matches was nothing new, though. Outbreaks of fighting at Millwall and West Ham, for example, were reported as far back as the 1930s. I can remember hearing about Millwall fans attacking a referee long before I started going to Chelsea. What was different was the scale. I have a mate, Dave, who is about ten years older than me, and he told me that the first time he saw trouble at a Chelsea game was in the mid '60s. They had travelled up to Nottingham to see Chelsea play Forest. There were no football specials then. The numbers travelling away didn't warrant it. Fighting, he said, hadn't entered their heads. They loved the team and that was all there was to it.

There were about a hundred Chelsea travelling that day,

including women and children and even members of players' families. They came off the train and walked down towards the Trent Bridge. Needless to say, there was no police, as there was no recognised problem then. Out of a pub appeared a large pack of Forest fans. They stood in front of the Chelsea, blocking their path, and made it clear they were going to attack anyone who tried to pass. The women and children were terrified but threaded their way through and were left alone. The young men and boys from London were left standing looking at the Forest fans. My mate said all this was new and they were not quite sure how to react. Then a Chelsea fan – I think he said his name was Norman – jumped up and drop-kicked the geezer standing at the front of the Forest fans. At that Greenaway let out a blood-curdling 'Zigger Zagger' and they chased the Forest fans all the way to the ground. My mate sees this as a defining moment in the history of the Chelsea gangs, but I suspect minor incidents like this were cropping up all over the land around this time.

By the early 1970s, any self-respecting team had a mob, with the likes of Chelsea, Manchester United, Spurs and Leeds boasting the highest numbers. Every London side, though, could muster a large hooligan element, as the London derbies would always attract the fair-weather thug. These were the boys who had no real sustained interest in football or football gangs but who would turn up at these games for the fighting that would always occur. The taking or attempted taking of ends was the vogue. Not many, though, took a serious pop at West Ham or Arsenal unless they had a death wish. Their reputations, among the mobs at least, went before them. Chelsea and Spurs had the numbers but didn't quite match the east and north Londoners on the fear scale. Palace, QPR and Charlton were all irrelevant.

But, of course, there was Millwall. The very name was enough to make the pleat on your Ben Sherman stand on end. Their mob was the most feared, but much of it was down to fear of the unknown. Millwall played in the lower divisions, so First Division clubs rarely came across them. If your club did have the misfortune of drawing them in one of the cup competitions, suddenly you were well gutted about not being able to go but you'd got a holiday booked with the girlfriend or your parents. Older boys found they had some pressing Saturday overtime they couldn't get out of. Millwall was a no-no.

FOUR

Shotguns and Hammers

In 1970 Chelsea got to another FA Cup final, and this time we won, beating Leeds United. I never made it to the final or the replay at Old Trafford but I vividly remember the morning after the replay. Our whole school was buzzing. Everyone turned up in their Chelsea scarves and hats, Chelsea songs rang out across the playground, and at one point we even lowered the school flag and replaced it with the Chelsea one. The headmistress joined in the spirit of it all by mentioning the victory in morning assembly. What a night that was, even for us kids, who celebrated just as enthusiastically without alcohol to fuel our emotions. The whole of south London was on a high. No more taking shit from the other boys; most of them had become born-again Chelsea fans anyway. The following season we beat the legendary Real Madrid to take the European Cup-Winners' Cup and we were the top kiddies. Bollocks to everyone else. Chelsea was where it was at. Peter Osgood, Charlie Cooke and Alan Hudson were the darlings of London and the King's Road was the centre of the universe.

The season after the FA Cup success, I was to go to that friendly and welcoming home of West Ham, Upton Park, for the first time. I was going with the Pollards Hill lot and around thirty of us met up at Beddington station. Some of us hadn't quite left school yet but there were a few older boys among us. One went by the name of Shotgun Boyce. His nickname he had awarded to himself on account of the banks he had held up at gunpoint. He told us that a twenty-year prison sentence had ensued. We were young but realised that to have committed these crimes and done the bird he must have nipped out of his playschool in the lunch hour, as he was barely in his twenties. Basically he was a harmless half-wit, and I suppose that was why he was hanging around with kids half his age.

Also with us that day was a fella called Les Kent. Now, Les had hit the big time, as his picture had appeared on the front cover of the hugely popular paperback book *Skinhead* written by Richard Allen. This book charted the violent life of a fictional skinhead who went by the name of Joe Hawkins. The book was fairly unbelievable pap but it sold thousands and spawned sequels such as *Suedehead* and *Boot Boys*. At one time dozens of tattered copies were being passed around at my school alone. Les's image on that front cover, lounging against a wall, hands behind his head, in full skinhead regalia, was one familiar to thousands of young people all over Britain. His fifteen minutes of fame were sweet; the birds mobbed him like a pop star. He held court at the Croydon Suite every Saturday morning, where they held a disco for the under-sixteens, often wearing exactly the same gear as in his cover picture to avoid any confusion. Jealous? Us? We told the girls he was our cousin and that he was not interested in the opposite sex as he was actually queer, so they were better off going out with us. It never did work.

We caught the overground to Wimbledon, where we met up with more Chelsea fans, and we all clambered aboard a District Line train to Upton Park. We were a smart crew dressed in our Levi cords, navy blue V-necked sleeveless jumpers and Ben Sherman shirts. There must have been about fifty of us now and Dave Perks, Keith Perland and Shotgun Boyce assumed control.

'When we get to the station,' ordered Shotgun, 'let everyone else off the train and then we walk to the ground together.'

Fairly obvious, I thought. Perhaps Shotgun had been getting his old lady to read him extracts of *Skinhead* at bedtime. Nevertheless, everyone listened intently, as these were the eldest and therefore presumably the best ruckers among us.

Perks, Perland and Boyce led us off the train at Upton Park

station and things immediately went boss-eyed. West Ham were waiting outside and steamed straight in without a word said. This was not a problem for us younger ones, who still had the knack of being able to blend in with our surroundings. We managed to walk away from the onslaught, singly or in pairs. West Ham thought either we were them or that we weren't worth hitting. It wasn't so easy for the older ones, especially poor old Shotgun, who was running for his life down the street, pursued by a baying mob. I couldn't help laughing as he bounded past us, mouth open in terror, looking like a cross between Herman Munster and the lead singer of Mungo Jerry.

The rest of us carried on to the ground, but we knew that once we had walked past the North Bank terrace, where the West Ham fans filed in, we would be easily identifiable as Chelsea. Trying to act nonchalant, we turned the corner into the road which led to the South Bank. West Ham again, and this time there were no older boys to absorb the assault. I suppose this was the first time I got smacked up at a football match, but I don't remember much about it. I backed myself up against the railings and closed my eyes as the boots and fists came raining in. Every one of us was taking a hiding and it seemed to go on forever. One solitary copper attempted to break up the fracas. They say there is never a policeman when you need one; well, I reckon we needed a hundred to get us out of that shit. How I wished I was swanning around the Croydon Suite now, on my own patch, with boys and girls of my own age, dancing to 'Spirit in the Sky'. I prayed to someone to get me out of this nightmare. I was sorry, God, please get me out of this, please.

Some of us managed to creep along the fence, and as the West Ham fans concentrated on kicking the prostrate boys of our number who had adopted the foetal position on the deck, we legged the last few yards to the gate. I leapt over the turnstile and into the ground. I've been chased out of grounds in my time but that was the only time I have ever been chased into one. Relief. Only now did I feel the bumps and bruises from the numerous blows to my head and legs, but I was safe for the time being. Ten or so of the Mitcham lot were also inside now. We were shocked and battered but strangely exhilarated. It was like a rite of passage. I now genuinely felt like one of the mob. We were flattered, in a way, that West Ham had bothered to give us a kicking.

Someone spotted Eccles standing alone at the top of the stairs. He was the bloke I had first seen marshalling the gangs at Tottenham. He was six foot tall and possibly ten years older than us. He came from Fulham and was unquestionably the recognised leader of the Chelsea gangs at the time. The sight of him lifted us. Dave Perks respectfully approached him.

'What's going on?'

'Fuck all,' replied Eccles, his lips barely moving. His face was redder than usual and he looked straight ahead as if we weren't there. He obviously wished we weren't. 'It's every man for himself. There is more West Ham in this end than Chelsea,' he added, speaking out of the side of his mouth like a bad ventriloquist. At that a huge gap opened up on the terrace and a menacing mob ducked under the crush barriers and headed towards us. The Chelsea behind us turned and fled; we could hear them. I looked to my side and saw the black Harrington jacket of Eccles disappearing down the stairs with the rest of them. We were back in the front line, us lot from Mitcham, and for some reason we did not run. The West Ham firm were facing us. They were grown men, not boys, and they were smiling and laughing at us.

''Ave a look. It's the facking Chelsea Double-Deckers,' mocked one, referring to a TV programme about a gang of kids that was showing at the time. Another eased himself under the last remaining crush barrier between them and us and lunged at me. Fortunately he stumbled forwards, and as he put his hands out to break his fall, Tony Aldworth volleyed him full in the face with his boot. This geezer was about thirty years of age and fifteen stone and already his eye was swelling up. West Ham paused. This wasn't in the plan – and neither was Teddy Adams, a big gypsy boy from Mitcham, encouraged by the West Ham hesitation, stepping forward into the no-man's land that had opened up and shouting, 'Come on then, mush, we'll have some.' The great thing about Mitcham boys was that many had gypsy blood in them and they feared no one, especially if they detected any lack of bottle in their opponents. In the meantime the police had arrived and placed a line of their finest between us and them. Heartened by the single strike and our stand, Chelsea fans gathered behind us and swelled our numbers. The ironic thing was that it was us kids on the front line who were now taking the piss out of West Ham and in particular Fatty, who was now sporting a shiner. We were on a high. Basically it had been a gang of schoolkids taking on West Ham's beer monsters and not doing too bad.

The walk back to the tube after the game was much safer, as the police seemed more effective in keeping the locals away from us. We could see and hear older Chelsea fans nudging one another and saying, 'They're the ones that fronted up West Ham.' Our little chests puffed out and our nervous walks transformed into a swagger. Talking to some older boys on the way home, we learned that the previous season a Chelsea firm from Stockwell had got in West Ham's North Bank, steamed straight in and cleared the end. When the east Londoners realised that there was only about a hundred Chelsea, they regrouped and ran them back out. Nevertheless, the Hammers had been humiliated and today's venom had all been about revenge.

Someone on the train claimed that Eccles had done a bunk just after half-time. I got to know him well in the years to come and he was no coward. He was a great architect of rucks, the best organiser and a maestro of taking ends, but for some reason he had no enthusiasm for mixing it with West Ham. It was like their mob had some strange hold over him. Perhaps it was because they had bigger and older chaps, or maybe he believed the reputation that went before them. Looking back on it now, it must have been hard for him. He was very well known and I don't think he enjoyed having that high a profile in London. You never knew who you were going to bump into when going about your normal business during the week. I went back to Upton Park many times over the next twenty years, and the lesson I learnt from that first time was that you've got to give it to them or they will eat you alive.

Back on Wimbledon station, who was waiting for us on the platform but Shotgun Boyce. He stood there by the snack bar, stuffing a whole bag of crisps into his mouth as fast as he could to avoid having to offer any around. As we walked towards him, someone rechristened him 'Starting Gun Boyce' because at the first sign of trouble he had been off like a shot.

Dave Perks switched his allegiance to West Ham a short time later. He claimed that Chelsea had mistaken him for a Hammer outside Stamford Bridge one afternoon and kicked shit out of him, so he decided to defect. I doubt it; I think he went because he was attracted by the tougher image that West Ham enjoyed in those days. Starting Gun Boyce drifted into oblivion, never appearing at football or the Croydon Suite again. One day, about fifteen years later, I spotted a man and wife jogging team running towards me on the Common. They wore identical purple shell-suits. A right couple of doughnuts. As they passed me, the gaping mouth and the long legs stirred a distant memory.

As the seasons passed, many of those Mitcham boys stopped going to football. Met a bird, got nicked, lost interest – a variety of reasons. Me, I kept on going. I left school and got a job with Dad and rarely saw the lads from Pollards Hill. All my money went on football, records and clothes. Reggae was the big thing, and in the early skinhead days anything on the Trojan record label was on the shopping list. I recall buying 'Return of the Django' by the Upsetters and 'The Liquidator', the latter becoming a theme tune down at the Bridge. The 'Tighten Up' albums were a must for all us young skins, and tracks like 'Wreck-a-Buddy' with the line 'and if he's ugly I don't mind/he's got a dick and I want a grind' were about the closest we got to sex.

My wages also afforded me the opportunity to expand my limited wardrobe. Jungle greens were meant to ride quite high up the leg but after three years of growing they were almost like shorts on me. I invested in a pair of two-tone tonic suits, one red and blue and the other green and blue. Dad helped me get started, as usual, and bought me a blue Crombie overcoat from a Jewish tailor in Petticoat Lane for fourteen shillings. With my steel comb nestling in the top pocket against a red silk handkerchief and liberal splashes of Brut aftershave, I thought I was the bollocks. Another accessory for milder weather was the Harrington jacket. These were wind-cheater jackets with a turned-up collar and a silky check lining. Running across the middle of the back was a wavy line. They were popularised by Ryan O'Neal, who played a character named Rodney Harrington in the American TV soap *Peyton Place*. Finally, perched on the head was a trilby-type hat known either as a blue beat hat or a pork pie hat. This headwear was particularly favoured by West Indian and African skinheads.

In the '60s and early '70s, black kids and white kids played together, danced together, drank together and went to football together. We liked the same music, clothes and clubs. There was no animosity whatsoever; in fact, black boys carried off the whole skinhead thing with style. Groups of us skinheads walked around Brixton Market and we wouldn't attract a second glance. We were young and rough but we were all on the same side. It wasn't until the mid to late '70s that these values changed, with the emergence of the far-right-wing groups that began to attract a following at football. Skinheads are indelibly associated with racism but in my mind history has been rewritten here. By the time race hate had emerged at football grounds, the original skinheads were a thing of the past. I must hold my hands up to one anomaly, though. Skinheads did go in for a spot of 'Paki-bashing', as it was called. It didn't last for long and it was carried out by both blacks and whites, as they victimised the first refugees from Idi Amin's Uganda. 'Pakis' were deemed fair game, as were homosexuals. 'Queer-bashing' was another short-lived but violent craze, latched onto by the press after a homosexual was kicked to death by a gang of skins on Wimbledon Common.

I had not been at work long when my dad sadly died. I was sixteen. It devastated me. I put a brave face on it and tried to be strong for Mum's sake, but inside I was aching and bitter. I treasure his memory, the trips to football, boxing and wrestling, the rattle he made me, the money he pressed into my palm even when Mum had said no, the laughs we had.

Only now do I appreciate how hard he worked for us and how he tried to make our lives happy and fulfilled. He was a good man, a real gent, and the best dad I could ever have wished for. God bless him. We will never forget. If I can be half the father to my kids that he was to me, then they will have been well served. With hindsight, his death affected me greatly. After that West Ham game when I thought I was Jack the Lad, if Dad had said, 'Look, Martin, I know what's happening at these football matches. I don't want you to get involved with any of this,' I'd have said, 'Okay, Dad' – and would have kept my promise.

FIVE

The Shit Years

After winning the FA Cup and the European Cup-Winners' Cup, the team began to decline. Slowly at first, but it soon gained momentum. A defeat in the FA Cup to Orient was the ultimate humiliation and the fans began to drift off. The club was pleading poverty and the star players like Osgood, Hudson and Cooke, along with the fans, were pissed off. It was rumoured that the club sold these Stamford Bridge favourites to pay the interest on the loan that had paid for the new stand that had been built. It seemed irrelevant that the club had no one to replace the team they were very publicly breaking up. I don't know if it was a conscious decision by all of us Mitcham boys to leave the football alone, but that is what happened for a time. There were other pastimes competing for our interest too. Drinking, chasing girls and watching live music began to take up our time. After a heavy Friday night on the piss, the last thing we wanted to do was wake up bright and early to catch a train from King's Cross to some poxy northern city. And missing out on the Saturday night opportunities at Tiffany's or Scamps didn't bear thinking about, although even at night spots like this, football-related brawls occasionally broke out.

One Friday night we were in Tiffany's in Wimbledon. The football season hadn't even started, but a group of Man United fans from the south London area were squaring up to a bunch of about twenty of Chelsea's main faces. Fortunately we were nothing to do with whatever had sparked the stand-off. We didn't want to get involved, as we knew both groups quite well. In fact, we had gone to school with some of the United boys.

Eccles was at the front of the Chelsea lot. It was strange to see him outside his normal environment. The bouncers wouldn't have let him in wearing his trademark Fred Perry, suede jacket and Levi cords. Instead he was wearing a jacket and tie and was surrounded by girls heavy with make-up who were dancing around their handbags, with soul music blaring out and strobe lights bathing the dance floor – instead of hundreds upon hundreds of fit young men marching around the industrial landscapes of northern England in T-shirts. He was like a fish out of water. Neither side looked like they would back down. We all settled on a line of bar stools, ordered our lagers and prepared to spectate at the inevitable row. A stocky Indian-looking geezer stepped forward out of the United gang and motioned for Eccles to do the same. At the same time the rest of the Cockney Reds took three paces forward. Diana Ross was whining in the background and the whole of Tiffany's, except the Chelsea firm, the United firm and us, were oblivious to the ritual being played out near the bar. Before Eccles could decide how to react, the bouncers moved in.

'Come on, Bob,' they said to the Indian-looking fella, whom they seemed to know. 'Save it for the terraces. Not here.'

The situation had been defused. No one had backed down and I think everyone was quite relieved. The Indian geezer walked over to us at the bar and shook hands with Bobby Reader and Peter Marney.

'What was that all about?' asked Bobby.

'Fuck all, really,' replied the Indian. 'Just Eccles being Eccles.'

Bobby then introduced me to the United fan.

'Martin, this is Bob, or Banana Bob to his friends.'

Banana Bob smiled and shook my hand. I found out later that he was probably better known as Bob the Wog, although I don't think his family called him that. Bob's main haunt was Scamps, a night-club in Sutton, and he was fast establishing himself as the main man among the United following in London. That night in Tiffany's he was accompanied by Dave

Griffin and Steve Prentice, whom I knew well. If things had got out of hand it would have been a close call to choose sides. I think I would have kept out of it, but I wouldn't have been surprised if some of our lot had teamed up with the United lot. There were unwritten rules and in those days you didn't carry over football rivalries into everyday life. You had to live and work with people all over London, whoever they were. If people had carried over their terrace wars to the building site, for example, London would never have been fully rebuilt after the war. Starting rows over football in clubs on your own doorstep was asking for trouble. Get into all that and you end up with people turning up at your house and the like. If Eccles's lot had started it, they should have known better. Some of our Mitcham gang were a bit cold to him anyway. He could be off-hand and was usually aloof. He was the leader of the Chelsea boys for a good few years but I'm not so sure he was democratically elected, if you know what I mean. Some of the leaders that came after him enjoyed the affection, as well as the respect, of their men.

It was around this time that we started to get a buzz from watching live bands. We even grew our hair long. From having no hair to long hair overnight. From skinhead to hippy – although we weren't hippies at all. We didn't walk around fields ringing bells, tripping on acid and urging peace on all and sundry. But we did grow the hair, get into new music and wear some pretty far-out gear – cheesecloth shirts (made in India) and brushed denim loons. We must have been mad to wear the fucking things. Trousers with a twenty-two-inch flare on board! I held out against it for as long as I could, but eventually you go with the flow. In between skinheads and all this, I had became a suedehead. A suedehead, though, was only a skin-head with a slightly longer barnet. Same clothes, same likes and dislikes.

One August weekend we decided to head off for the Reading rock festival, which was a three-day event. We'd been the previous year and camped out with the real old hairies, freezing our bollocks off at night. This year we decided to do it in comfort, hiring a cabin cruiser from Walton-on-Thames and sailing along the waterway all the way to the festival, which was in a magical location next to the river. The plan was that five of us would pick up the boat from the owners and then a mile or two upstream we would collect the rest of our crowd. The owners were satisfied that we were nice boys and told us proudly that Cliff Richard had once owned the boat.

'Really?' I said, keeping a straight face. 'He's always been a hero of mine.' I turned to the others, who were also trying not to laugh. 'I could be the first boy to sleep in his bed.'

We all rolled up laughing. The owners looked at us like we were raving nutters and ignored our mirth to show us the workings of the boat. No one was taking a blind bit of notice but we got moving and they waved us off. We picked up the others as planned, and now a six-berth boat was carrying twelve. We were the original boat people. Inevitably we soon got a tug from the river police for jumping the queue at a lock.

'There are rules on the river,' the copper warned us, 'and you boys are overloaded.'

I explained that there were only five of us and that the other seven were hitchhikers we had picked up at the last lock. 'They're getting off at the next lock,' I assured them, and they seemed happy enough with that.

We arrived in Reading in one piece, the boat and us, and we looked forward to seeing all the bands on the bill. The Sensational Alex Harvey Band, Cockney Rebel, Hawkwind and a variety of other headbanging groups were all to feature over the weekend. A few of the boys had bought some puff and pills from some Taffies. I didn't mind a blow but you wouldn't catch me taking a pill in a million years. Even as a kid, Mum would have to get me in a headlock that Mick McManus would have been proud of just to get a junior aspirin down me. She would bend my nose back until I opened my mouth, ram the pill down my throat and then close my jaws up until I'd swallowed. I can't remember now what pills we scored but it was probably French blues at three for fifty pence. The blues were speed, which made the half of our group who were popping them talk incessantly at the other half, who weren't listening because they were chilling out from smoking a whacking great clump of black Moroccan. Experienced drug users would know that whizz and blow don't mix, but we never did anything the way you were supposed to.

The puff obviously affected my sense of judgement, because on the last day I followed the others on a tour of the clothes stalls that were dotted all around the site. I like to think I was stoned but like a prize div I bought a mauve, pink and white checked cheesecloth number and blue brushed denim loons. The last night of the concert was the bollocks and we headbanged and freaked out with the best of them until the sun came up. Nothing was further from our minds than having a row at football. From 'Kill the Bill' to 'Give peace a chance'.

Heading back down the river, like good boys we scrubbed and cleaned the boat until it sparkled. The owners trusting us with such a tasty piece of equipment was a new experience and we wanted to repay that trust. They were obviously a bit jittery about letting us loose with their asset because when we got back we could see their surprise at the condition in which we had returned it. They were so pleased that they took us back to Wimbledon train station in their car.

Before I had left the boat I had slipped into my new gear. As you do with any new clobber, I studied myself in the mirror, turning this way and that, swivelling my head over my shoulder to see how I looked from behind. Did it look okay? We're worse than fucking women, us blokes. I arrived home and walked into the front room, forgetting that I had left a couple of days before as a suedehead. Mum, my brother Alan and his wife were engrossed in the television.

'All right, boy?' asked Alan, not moving his eyes from the box.

'Great. What's for tea, Mum?'

The old girl looked up and slowly a huge grin swept across her face.

'I didn't know I had a daughter. What the fucking hell are you wearing?'

With that my brother dragged himself away from Reg Varney, turned around in his armchair and looked me up and down. He and his missus just cracked up laughing.

'Fuck me, if it ain't Quentin Crisp.'

'Who's Quentin Crisp?'

'The queen of the sausage jockeys,' explained Alan, still pissing himself with laughter. 'Don't tell me,' he continued, 'you've been to Reading, you and all yer mates have got right into it and you've walked round and bought all the clobber.'

'How d'you know?' I asked, feeling injured by being the figure of fun in my own house.

'Because I was a silly prick once too! You should ask me first and learn from my mistakes. That way you'll make less of a prat of yerself.' He had stopped laughing now. 'I never thought I'd see the day, you turning fucking hippy. I s'pose you've been sitting round the campfire smoking the pipe of peace, have you?'

Not wishing to get into this in front of Mum, I didn't answer.

'And by the way, go and have a bath.'

'Why?'

'Because you fucking stink.'

I slammed the door and went up to the bathroom. I was puzzled why he had turned a bit nasty. Perhaps he was trying to look out for me. I can recall Dad having a right go at him when he was my age. Beatnik, I think he called him.

Later that night Alan apologised for taking the piss.

'I'm just trying to warn you about the dangers of smoking cannabis,' he explained.

'Well, you fucking smoked it,' I retorted.

'Exactly. I smoked the fucking stuff for years. There's a lot of pros and cons to it and you should know about it, that's all. I read a report once that said it can fuck your memory right up.'

'Really?'

'Yep. I've even written a book about the whole subject, so I should know.'

'A book? Where is it, then? I've never seen it.'

'No, I can't find it. Can't remember where I left it. Well, I think I wrote a book. I ain't too sure.'

A wicked smile lit up his face. The bastard was winding me up again and we both creased up laughing.

Not long after, Peter Stevens and I were doing some building work round my Mum's house when there was a knock at the door. In trooped Bobby Reader with ten of the boys.

'Coming to football, you two?'

'Who's playing?' I asked.

'We've got Fulham in a pre-season friendly.'

Having laid off for a while, Bobby had suddenly decided there was novelty value in going to a match and had rung around all our crowd.

'See ya later, Ma,' I shouted as we downed tools and left yet another job half-done.

'Typical,' she chided me. 'You start something and never finish it.'

'I'll be back in a fortnight.'

As we walked through Hadfields Park on the way to the game, we talked about Chelsea. Most of us agreed that we didn't fancy going regularly, what with all the star talent going and the way the team was performing. 'The fucking club don't deserve supporters,' I said, and I wondered aloud whether there would soon be a club left to support, what with all the financial troubles and that. One of the Manning twins said I was fucking cheerful. I replied that I was happy that football was no longer the be-all and end-all of my life. Quickly, though, something happened that made me realise it wasn't just what went on *on* the pitch that had made me go to football anyway. One of the boys at the front had spotted two well-known Yids from Richmond at the bus stop up ahead. We devised a plan to trap them. Two of the boys whom the Yids wouldn't have known from Adam walked across the road and waited at the stop behind them. The rest of us jumped on a bus to Morden, hung on for five minutes at the bus terminal and then jumped on the bus that would pass the bus stop where the Yids were waiting. Everything was falling into place. We could see them ahead so we all sat in seats scattered around the top deck of the bus. The doors opened and up the stairs they came.

'Hello, tosspots,' said Bobby.

The Yids sussed it straight away and turned to go back down

the spiral staircase, but our two boys were jammed up behind them, blocking any escape.

'Come on up, boys, and make yourself comfortable.'

The look on their boats said it all. Fear mixed with anger at finding themselves in this situation. These two were normally a trappy pair of ponces who thought they were something at Spurs. Like most Tottenham boys, they had all the bunny when they outnumbered you but were shrinking violets when the tables were turned.

'Where are you off to, chaps? Boys Brigade? Scouts? Cubs? Girl Guides?'

They went redder and redder. One of them was gripping the seat rail hard in an attempt to stop his hand shaking. Anger and fear. We carried on taking the piss all the way to Wimbledon station, and not once did they answer back. They just stared straight ahead. Being gentlemen, we were only giving them a squeeze, a warning; that was enough. The next time we saw them at football or in a pub or club, they would know we had one over on them. I seriously doubt if they would have extended the same courtesy to us.

We walked through the park down towards Craven Cottage, taking off our shirts and basking in the August sunshine. It was a beautiful day for watching football, even if it was only a meaningless match. So different from standing in a hostile northern khazi, warming your hands on oxtail soup in a plastic cup. Those cricket boys have got the right idea. Play when it is nice and warm. Fuck the cold weather. Ripples of applause and tea and biscuits at half-time.

There would be no trouble today. No way. Fulham don't have a mob, and if they did they would be indistinguishable from the Chelsea boys. Many of Chelsea's top and oldest faces lived in Fulham. You don't smash up your own back yard and fight with your old schoolmates. Although a couple of years on Chelsea did just that. Came out of Craven Cottage and demolished the Fulham Palace Road. That was when Chelsea was attracting every half-wit vandal residing in the south-east of England. A lot of the original Chelsea firm were very pissed off about that.

Everyone was congregating outside the ground, renewing acquaintances and catching up on gossip. We bumped into lots of familiar faces, some we had not seen for a couple of years now. Where had we been hiding, they wanted to know. Too busy drinking and shagging, we told them. They gave us funny looks, as if we were the ones who needed our brains tested. Surely there was no contest between having your spinning head buried in a soft pair of tits on a Saturday night and having your swede smashed by a copper's truncheon in a Nottingham backstreet?

It was comforting to note that we weren't the only ones dressed like late returnees from Woodstock. Even the black boys had got the hippy bug, wearing Jimi Hendrix-style hair: five foot high and two foot either side of each lughole like some huge, fuzzy, black crash-helmet.

Inside the ground, I couldn't believe the support Chelsea had. All sides of the ground were crammed with blue and white, all here to watch the usual pre-season garbage and a team that didn't deserve such devotion. After the game we headed back to the Nag's Head at Mitcham Fairgreen for a night on the piss. A stripper strutted her stuff and passed the hat around but we weren't watching. We were too busy arranging to go down to Southampton for Chelsea's first away of the season. We had the bug again.

On the day of the game we caught a bus to Surbiton, from where we picked up the slow train down to Southampton. When I say slow, I mean slow. It stopped at every fucking ramshackle shed imaginable. What was normally a two-hour dash turned into a five-hour nightmare. Some of these stations had not seen human life for years, let alone a train. On each platform stood a member of the Will Hay fan club, blowing his little whistle and almost orgasming over our arrival.

When we finally got there, we hit the first pub, which was chocker with Chelsea. We recognised a lot of our old chums. I had a chat with Skitzy, who had been going to Chelsea as long as I had. His nickname summed him up. He was a very quiet fella but when at football he loved a tear-up, and he could really hold his hands up. Mind you, on one occasion I saw him struck speechless. By Tommy Docherty, of all people. It was not long after Tommy had fallen out with Manchester United over having an affair with the wife of one of the members of staff. We were all standing on the concourse at Euston station, loading up on newspapers, fags and sweets for our away journey. Tommy Doc had just got off a train and was striding purposefully over to us and the exits.

'Hello, Tom. Still pumping up Mary Brown?' said Skitzy as the former Chelsea manager drew level. He stopped, put his holdall on the floor, swung around and flew over to us. He put his face right up against Skitzy's and said in a thick Scottish accent, 'What d'ya fucking say?' Poor old Skitz was dumb-founded; Docherty looked like he was about to explode. Beads of sweat bubbled up on his forehead as he awaited Skitzy's response. Fortunately for all concerned, after a few worrying seconds he picked up his luggage and trounced off, muttering to himself.

Outside a Southampton pub, someone was shouting and bawling to get the crowd moving down to the ground. Still crazy after all these years. It was Greenaway, acting as an unelected steward. I could never make him out. To be a leader you needed to be able to flex a bit of muscle now and then, but I never saw Greenaway in action. I never saw him even threaten to throw a punch. He sang with some aggression, though – until he was blue in the face and the sweat poured over on to his customary collar and tie. For some reason he insisted on wearing a jacket, collar and tie to Chelsea. He was a most unlikely leader, but then I don't think he even saw himself that way. He was Mr Chelsea who could have gone on Hughie Green's *Double your Money* and won answering questions on the history of the club. And the fans were his flock. It didn't matter to him that so many were wayward. They were Chelsea and that was good enough for him.

At one time his 'Zigger Zagger' chant was the best-known football mantra in the country. To my mind he was the Tony Hatch or Mickie Most of the Shed, a conductor of singing rather than an instigator of violence. His efforts, though, definitely won Chelsea games. He got everyone singing aloud, getting behind the team, willing them to win – or, nowadays, to at least equalise. These performances completely exhausted him. There was no way he could muster enough strength for a fight after the game even if he had wanted to. He was probably Chelsea's truest supporter and the club should have honoured him rather than regarded him as some hooligan crank. Some years later, after a lively excursion down to Brighton, a Sunday tabloid did a job on him. In typical bully-boy style, they libelled and demonised him, confident he did not have the means to fight back. That so-called exposé was a big blow to Greenaway personally.

In those days it was the done thing to stand on the home fans' end. If the hosts couldn't shift you either by force or by psyching you out, you had taken their end. Some grounds just accepted that we'd be in the home end and left it at that; others at least put up a fight; and just a few drove us out. Here in the Milton Road end, the Old Bill didn't seem to give a fuck; they were just standing around chatting. We were where we shouldn't be and they ignored us. A fight broke out further up the terrace and we got shoved down to the front. Turning to face the direction of the trouble, all we could see was more and more Chelsea tumbling down the terrace. Everyone was getting squashed and we were being forced over to the corner flag. Whoever was pushing down from the top, Saints fans or Old Bill, they were certainly taking the end back under control. People were calling out to 'Stand, stand'. Against whom? All we could see was Chelsea. There had been no roar and no chants. But as the main part of the end fanned out a bit, the red and white scarves came out from under jumpers and knee-length cardigans. The Saints had got their end back. Sneakily, though. Some Chelsea were even on the pitch now, in the corner. This was a bit embarrassing, so we took a firm up to the top of the terrace away from where all the action and the police were. We soon came across a mob who seemed to be orchestrating the trouble from on high. A boss-eyed, nasty-looking wanker saw us approaching.

'Whatya running for, Chelsea? Can't you handle it?'
Everyone turned around to back Clarence up.

'Come on, Chelsea,' chipped in another. 'Let's do it. We're not Southampton, we're Bournemouth's firm.'

'No,' I sighed in mock disbelief. 'I thought you might have been a real tasty firm like Watford or Northampton.'

We could also see now that it was the Old Bill who were forcing Chelsea over into the corner, not Saints fans. They were simply stepping into the space the police were creating. Now it all made sense. The Bournemouth big-mouth squad turned and ran as soon as they realised we weren't going anywhere and the police then charged us lot back down to the corner flag. The pressure in this section of the ground was so great now that everyone had to spill on to the pitch. The police surrounded us and escorted us down the side of the pitch to our rightful end. Southampton burst into song: 'Chelsea ran from Southampton!' We turned around and gave them the wankers sign. Stepping over the terrace into the uncovered end which held the bulk of the travelling Chelsea army, we were given the customary round of applause for operating inside enemy lines.

The teams ran out on to the turf and Peter Osgood, now playing for Southampton, was met by boos and jeers and the chant of 'Osgood, was good, now he's no good'. Some were even calling him Judas. Short memories. In my opinion he was the greatest player ever to wear a Chelsea shirt. Some accused him of laziness and said his heart wasn't in Chelsea. Bollocks. He was a genius. I was converted the day I first sang 'Osgood, Osgood, born is the king of Stamford Bridge' as an apprentice Shed boy. He scored blinding goals with his feet and his head. But most of all he had this aura about him. He glided around the pitch as if his feet weren't touching the ground. I loved him. Even the old man, who, like all older men, thought his generation of players was better than the current crop, thought Osgood was the dog's bollocks. Strangely, though, he considered Ronnie 'Chopper' Harris a skilful player who should have been in the England team. I watched Ronnie for years and loved him to death but, sorry Dad, skill was not one of his attributes. In the twilight of his career Ossie returned to the Bridge and I remember him scoring our only goal in a 7–1 drubbing up at Middlesbrough. They were sad times for Chelsea. The only consolation that day was that about a hundred of us left the match ten minutes early and walked around Ayresome Park to the home end and cleared it.

After the game Southampton did their usual disappearing act and all that was left was for the Chelsea fans to get out into the streets and wreck the gaff in their usual pathetic way. These divvies used the numbers to smash bus shelters, shop windows and cars and generally scare grannies and small kids. We had nothing to do with this lot; at the first whiff of a mob they'd be dust. Their only rule was 'if it don't hit back – smash it'. They really did give the ruckers a bad name. We were at the tail end of this tidal wave of destruction that day and couldn't believe the scale of the vandalism. Every window in and around the station had been smashed, doors ripped off their hinges and cars overturned. It could have been Beirut instead of Southampton. These were the true hooligans. They didn't hold their hands up, yet the press liked to group us together under the same banner: hooligans and thugs. I was neither.

A few weeks later we were off to the Midlands for a match that promised more of a decent ruck – Wolverhampton Wanderers. They were normally game. They had no away mob in London but at home they tried their best to get at you. We were all working on a building site at the time and the day before the game Bobby Reader decided that he knew where we could pinch some drink for the trip up to Noddy Holderland. He climbed over a fence at the bottom of the site and tiptoed along the alley on the other side; meanwhile, we were all hanging over the fence watching him. After ages of rearranging crates of empties at the back of an off-licence, he came running back to us and passed up a box full of bottles.

'What we got, Bob?' asked someone excitedly.

'Fuck knows.'

Bobby, who had followed his old man into bricklaying, was the daredevil among us. I'd known him since the first day of infant school, where he was not only the class clown but the school one as well. There was never a dull moment with Bob around.

Peter Marney, another brickie and one of our Chelsea firm, looked in the cardboard box and burst out laughing.

'Sherry! Fucking dry sherry! That's what he's half-inched.'

Nevertheless we stashed it and picked it up in the morning to take on the football special up to Wolverhampton. Twelve bottles of the stuff, and it tasted the business out of those little brown plastic British Rail cups. We got some weird looks from the rest of the travellers, all knocking back their cans of Watney's Pale Ale and big bottles of cider, and there we were sipping dry sherry with our little fingers raised in the air. They must have been thinking, 'These Surrey boys have got some class. It must be right posh where they live.' To cap it all, we were one of the first lots to wear full-length leather trench coats. These had been made fashionable by the *Shaft* films about a black American detective. What with the long hair, the tank top jumpers and the SS coats, we must have stood out like sore thumbs. If dry sherry is what they drink at dinner parties, I don't know how these rich people don't end up ripping each other's heads off, because by the time we'd each got a bottle of that warming up our guts we were raring to go.

The police escorted us from the station to the ground. Rumour on the train was that just before the ground there was a subway and that was where Wolves would normally try to ambush the visiting fans. They called themselves the 'Subway Army' for a while. We pushed ourselves to the front, as did all the usual suspects. Ruckers at the front, property destroyers in the middle and singers, women and children at the back. We saw the subway up ahead and the whole train-load let out a chant of 'Chelsea!'. If Wolves were the other side, they'd certainly know we were here.

We're now in the subway and we're nice and tight. Quite often with Chelsea the mob gets strung out, but tales of the subway have caused us to stick well together. Halfway through the tunnel and still no sign – but then they are in front of us. A big old black and white mob. The police at the front raise their hands for us to stop, like Roman generals leading a column of legionaries. That sherry must have really taken effect, because we think that wave means 'Get into the wankers!'. We're straight through the Old Bill and chasing Wolves away. Packs of them. Everyone in the tunnel is roaring and the echo makes it sound like five thousand, not five hundred. No wonder they're sprinting. More police arrive and get it under control. The Wolves mob are across the road and now, in the light, I can see them clearly. To my surprise, many of them are Asian. This is the first time I've seen Asian kids in a football mob. The police take us the last leg to the ground. The Wolves follow on the other side of the road but make no serious attempt to break the police line. Outside the turnstile we are all searched. A copper asks if I have been drinking. 'Only dry sherry,' I reply, and he just smiles as if I am taking the piss.

The support today is not massive. A thousand at the most. Normally three to four would have travelled. But what can you expect when your club sells all your players and fields a youth team? Wolves score from practically the first touch of the ball and there are locals all around jumping up and down. 'What's going on here?' we think. A fight breaks out and a gap appears between us and a little firm of Wolverhampton. One motions me towards him. I plant one on his chin and he goes down like a sack of spuds. See, those lessons at Mitcham Boxing Club did pay off after all, Mum! The rest of them go on the missing list. The Old Bill come galloping in, looking for someone to nick, but we're experts at pretending we're there to watch football. We look out at the game. Fools them every time. The game ends 7 fucking 1. Chelsea losing 7–1 to Wolverhampton, who only have an ageing Derek Dougan to their name! No one is up for a fight either, not outside the ground, nor even at the dreaded subway. Carry on like this and we'll end up in the Second Division.

SIX

Malice in Sunderland

There was a song released in the early 1970s by jack-of-all-trades, master of none Jonathan King, under the pseudonym of the Piglets. The song was called 'Johnny Reggae' and was famous (for fifteen minutes) for the then hugely suggestive line 'Johnny, Johnny Reggae/Johnny, Johnny Reggae/Johnny Reggae/Lie on me'. More significantly, for me at least, the song heralded a whole new dress culture. Out went Dr Martens, Ivy loafers, box Gibsons, smooth Levi sta-prests, Ben Shermans and most of the other badges of the skinhead era. They were replaced by baseball boots, stars and stripes T-shirts, Levi denim jackets, flowered shirts with dodgy large collars and Rupert the Bear checked trousers which would later grow into the even more laughable Oxford bags. Not many months later those '70s trademarks platform shoes and Budgie jackets also arrived. The coming of Gary Glitter, T-Rex, Slade, the Sweet and the associated glam rock movement prompted many of these fashion changes. These bands filled the void left by the Beatles, who had split following a Japanese invasion, and the Stones, who were lounging around in the south of France contemplating their tax status.

For fortysomethings who lived through this era and were not individual enough to resist being a dedicated follower of fashion, this was a bad time. Most of us would rather not think about it, let alone talk about it. Skinhead gear was over-the-top macho, agreed, but this look was unbelievable. Skinhead fashion survives to this day, swimming in and out of style, and in many cases has crossed over into mainstream dress. But this '70s clobber has practically disappeared altogether, which says a lot. Even Carlisle fans have binned their surfing beads and scraped the glitter spots away from under their eyes, I am told. Seriously, how could you have a row at football dressed like a shirtlifter? When a fight broke out you couldn't be sure whether you were trading punches with a boy or a girl! I don't know if many rucks from those periods have survived on film, but if they have, they must be hilarious: people clumping each other with pathetic silk scarves hanging from their wrists, shielding their eyes from those lethal pointed collars but keeping their heads still so as not to mess up their new Rod Stewart feather-cuts. I look back on those times as the hooligan pink period.

Trouble, though, did continue, although some sort of calm had descended after the initial shock-horror reactions of the late '60s. People now expected trouble at football and the press had made the problem their own. Around this time much was being written about the 'scourge' of the game, but it was totally out of proportion with what was going on. The authorities had tightened up and no First Division game went off without a massive police presence. The pretence of anarchy attracted more and more people, and the legends and fantasy began to filter down the urban-myth chain to school playgrounds up and down the country. Accounts of fights were embellished as they were passed along the grapevine until there were huddles of schoolchildren in their comprehensive-school classrooms loudly discussing riots that had never taken place. Mental pictures of leaders were constructed that bore no resemblance to the original article. But, for the media, it was all good copy, and the press rushed out to over-report outbreaks of violence (their words, not mine) and interview the so-called hooligans. They published league tables based on arrests and profiled strangely named thugs whom no one had ever heard of and who were in all probability completely fictional.

The hooligans, meanwhile, had allowed themselves to become institutionalised. They arrived at grounds, dutifully went in their own ends, sang songs and threw insults at the opposing supporters. After the match they would make their way home whilst posturing again at the other team's fans but making no real attempt to outmanoeuvre the police and get at them. It was loud and rowdy and gates were high, but the first wave of skinhead-driven football violence had subsided into a phoney war situation in those first few years of the decade.

Meanwhile, Chelsea's glory days were over for the foreseeable future. The FA Cup and European Cup-Winners' Cup successes seemed an age ago, most of the star names had faded or gone, and the crowd, whilst still passionate, was dwindling. Eventually, by the end of 1974–75, the unthinkable happened and Chelsea were relegated to the old Second Division. Strangely, this seemed to excite many Chelsea fans. A whole load of new grounds, new towns and new opposition. There was an unconscious decision taken by Chelsea supporters to follow the club up and down the land with renewed fervour, regardless of the reduced circumstances.

I was working on a building site that summer when the *Evening News* came in with the coming season's fixtures. First game Sunderland away. Roker Park. That'll do. That's all we talked about for the next few weeks. Chelsea were sure to take thousands. We were not disappointed. Arriving at King's Cross station at 7.30 a.m., we saw that British Rail were running two football specials. The previous season, one had been the norm. The specials were non-service trains which were used to enable football fans to travel cheaply to away games. Not that they were really for our benefit; the idea was that they knew where we were, what time we were leaving and what time we were arriving. Of course, it had the added bonus of keeping us away from respectable people. And we got what we paid for. The rolling stock was old – barely rolling – and dirty. Normally there was no heating and there was certainly no buffet, but we could live with that. Greenaway organised this travel for a few seasons. He called his scheme 'CAT' – an acronym for Chelsea Away Travel – and had pretty coloured tickets printed up. It made him happy, anyway.

Our group was on the first special out so we climbed aboard and walked along inside the train until we found some seats.

Every table was piled high with beer, mainly cans of Long Life, and most tables were kicking off the usual card schools that helped pass the time. Money was already changing hands. The non-gamblers had their noses buried in the *Sun* or the *Mirror* and the odd pisshead tried to sleep, head wedged against the window, after a heavy Friday night. Against a background noise of the hissing of ring-pulls, we settled down in our seats to begin some serious banter. This was our way of filling the time. Silly to get pissed. Headache by the time you get there. No enthusiasm for the dinnertime session and in no fit state for a ruck. Read a paper? The *Sun* and the *Mirror*? Done before the train has left the platform. Wouldn't have the front to buy the *Telegraph*, but at least there would have been something to read. No, we just sat there and dug each other out. The previous night, the ugly bird, the clothes, the family, the job, the past, whatever. It was all harmless and enter-taining.

Finally we arrive at Seaburn Station near Sunderland and the local Old Bill are out in force to greet us. It is a short walk to the ground and for our own protection, apparently, the police will accompany us to the stadium. We push out through the station doors as one and are milling around the forecourt area. The police line has already broken and the escort is no more. Just a hundred yards in front of us is a pub and outside stand scores of today's enemy, happily knocking back cloudy bitter in their red and white striped shirts. Without a word, the Chelsea fans run straight at the pub, some no doubt in need of a drink but most for a welcome but unexpected early row. Sunderland act fast and bolt back inside the pub. It is like watching a film of a crowd of people leaving a building being shown backwards and speeded up. A dozen or so pause for a couple of seconds to knock back their drinks before scamper-ing or try to stroll back in rather than run so as not to compromise their image. Bad move. They take the full brunt of the fists and boots of the first twenty or so marauding Chelsea. Like animals under the wheels of a car, within seconds they are sucked beneath the thundering herd. The pub door won't open. Sunderland are desperately trying to hold it closed from the inside. A big guy puts his foot up against the wall, grabs the handle and yanks it open. We are inside.

We automatically fan out to allow as many of our boys to get through the entrance as quickly as possible. Our eyes dart everywhere, wary of flying glasses or a sneaky pool cue over the head. 'Come on, Sunderland! Come on, then!' we shout between gritted teeth. We are beckoning them towards us, legs apart with both hands outstretched from the waist. Behind us the hordes have destroyed the fixtures and fittings in seconds. The plate-glass windows have all gone in, tables and chairs have been turned over – mainly by fleeing Sunderland drinkers – and Chelsea are lobbing glasses at the optics and the mirrors. It is pandemonium. Almost as quickly as we have burst in, the home fans have burst out the back exit, followed by the terrified landlord and his staff. Half-smoked cigarettes are balanced on ashtrays along the bar. I step on a vintage Guinness toucan mirror which has fallen from the wall. 10cc are playing on the jukebox, assuring us they are not in love. They should rename this boozer the Marie Celeste. Or the No Bottle and Glass. There is also no Sunderland, but we have been joined by the police, who, embarrassed by their doziness, get busy nicking any Londoners holding bottles or glasses. They can hardly argue that they have just been served. The rest of us are bundled back out on to the path and are shoved in the general direction of the ground. No real escort again. Strange.

We turn a corner and before us is a fresh Sunderland mob, bobbing up and down two hundred yards away. Almost shadow boxing.

'Slow down at the front!' barks Eccles. 'Let the ones at the back catch up.'

Sensible. The bobbing up and down throws us a bit. They're like hungry boxers standing in their corners, waiting for the bell to ring. It looks like this little lot are definitely up for it. I think this is why the Old Bill have disappeared – they are hoping we cop a good hiding.

'Right, everyone stick together,' urges another voice at the front.

'Walk towards them. Don't run – just walk.'

Eccles again. We do as we are told and slowly stroll towards the mob ahead of us. Slow-motion time again. A hundred yards now and still no uniforms. A whole special load of Chelsea and roughly the same amount of them. Seven hundred apiece, I reckon. That's a big off. Fifty yards.

'Spread out,' orders Eccles, 'and walk, don't run.'

They haven't run.

Bobby Reader reads my mind.

'They're a bit game. It don't look like they're going to move.'

Suddenly a roar goes up and from alleyways on both sides of us are more of their mob, steaming into us from the flanks. Boots and fists are flying, but we don't run and this worries them. The element of surprise over, we go back into them. For some reason the mob in front have not taken advantage of their ambush tactics and do not attack us full on. Looks to me like the whole of Sunderland has turned out to bash a cockney. But it's us bashing them, as we chase the bushwhackers back up the alleys and turn and charge, full thrust, at the main crew. They're not having any of it now; they spin around and have it on their toes. We chase for about a mile, capturing the odd one who wants to make a stand and fight, but they are quickly run over by the rampant Chelsea invaders. One bloke stops, turns and faces us. The lads in front just run past him. I notice he's got a messy Indian ink borstal tattoo on his cheekbone and he's waving his fists around. They too are covered in faded blue ink. 'What's wrong with these northerners?' I'm thinking. 'Even their tattoos are homemade and drab.' A black Chelsea guy throws a punch but misses and someone else moves in on his blind side and nuts him cleanly. He's down.

Outside the home end of Roker Park, the remainder of the mob stop as they gain confidence from some fresh faces hanging around. We stop too, catch our breath, regroup and start to walk towards them. This time there are no commands but we know it is right to run at them and we do. They flee and clamber over the turnstiles into the ground with us in hot pursuit. They are joined now by yet another crowd of Sunderland supporters who have been watching the events from the top of the steps in their home end. The police's blind-eye policy has gone boss-eyed. Our hiding has not materialised. They put themselves between us and the Sunderland and block off the home turnstiles. Then they lead us down the side of the ground to the visiting fans' end and we pay our money and climb the steps up on to the open terracing.

At the top a fight has broken out and people are getting pushed back down the steps on top of us. One of our lot, Peter Stevens, shouts, 'Get yer arses up here quick! The bastards are this end too.' We leap up the terrace, four or five stairs at a time. At the top Peter is clumping a big fat northerner who goes down and other Chelsea boys kick him across the concrete. We follow down the steps, lashing out at any Sunderland fan who dares square up – and there are a few. The police, who have been several moves behind events all day, force another line between the two groups. Peace is restored. That gives us the opportunity to allow the top faces to get to the front, ready for the next off. Eccles and his boys push forwards first, hands in pockets, feigning disinterest. Then Babs and his gang shove through alongside them.

Babs was well known to all Chelsea fans even by then. Game as anything, he would back down from no one in a fight at football. He was a stocky fella but was disadvantaged against other blokes on account of having only one arm. But that didn't stop him from having a tear-up. Far from it. I think it made him all the more determined not to take a backwards step. That day in Sunderland he was wearing jeans and a thin grey cotton polo neck. In winter he wore a green combat jacket. He always looked smart. I was to get to know Babsy well over the years and found him to be a friendly bloke who was always cheerful and approachable. He would often ask what you'd been up to and how you were. His followers would have died for him (some nearly did), such was the loyalty he inspired.

We're a bad-breathed policeman away from the Sunderland and one lump stands out among them like a sore thumb. He has taken his shirt off and is bare-chested, whilst making himself well busy. At every opportunity he leans through the police cordon and delivers a resounding punch or kick to the nearest Chelsea fan, who, on retaliating, is thrown out or even nicked. The Old Bill conveniently don't notice him and he smiles in the knowledge that his local constabulary hates cockneys almost as much as he does. This pattern is a feature of travelling up north. You are a target for the city's police force. They nick you for anything but allow the local yobs to run amok. So you're not only up against the town's thugs, but you're also being picked on by the police for being a Londoner. We are cocky and we are troublemakers and we need to be taught a lesson. A beating by the local lads ideally, but a nicking will do.

This Sunderland wanker has a very noticeable smile, as most of his teeth are missing. We verbal him up about his film-star looks and this irks him more than being chinned, I reckon. Mind you, they all look suspect. As I say, most of Sunderland has turned out, the crowd consisting of skinheads, greasers, beer monsters, child molesters and trainspotters. You name it, they are following the local side today.

Chelsea have taken an early lead on the pitch and this prompts some scattered pockets of fighting. We use this diversion to sneak through the police divide. It is quite a surprise for the Sunderland fans that twenty or so Chelsea boys have appeared right behind them. The Old Bill are oblivious to our presence and resume watching the match. A few of the fans begin to shuffle nervously down the terracing and a space of about ten feet opens up. One of their boys walks cautiously towards us. He stands in front of me, his body language not one of confrontation.

'Howsit going, mate?' he asks in a southern accent.

'Not bad,' I nod suspiciously. I'm trying to work out what a southerner is doing in here with their firm.

'Cor, you lot are a bit game,' he offers up.

Bobby Reader pushes in front of me and stares deep into the bloke's eyes.

'Hold on. I don't want any trouble. I've just come over for a chat with you guys.'

Us guys? Who does he think he is – Tony Blackburn? He's frightened now.

'A fucking chat!' sneers Tony Aldworth.

'What d'you wanna chat about?' asks another.

'Well, tell your mob to form an orderly queue and we'll chat to them one by one,' chips in Tony.

'No, don't take the piss, boys. I only wanted to tell you that the only other team ever to come here and hold their own are the Geordie bastards from up the road.'

I suspect he means Newcastle. Flattery will get you nowhere, I'm afraid.

'What you doing with that lot?' I enquire, nodding at the Sunderland boys still a safe distance behind this would-be Henry Kissinger. He explains that he lives in Dover, his mother's family are from Sunderland and he has travelled up to stay with cousins who have brought him to the game. Being from the south of England, it seems, gives him the right to intercept a serious off.

I advise him, 'Better tell yer cousins to take you home a bit lively, because when the game's finished all you lot are going to get bashed, so fuck off.'

With that, a fist from behind me flashes past my cheek and smashes into his mouth. He staggers back down the terrace holding his face. Their boys have seen this but make no move to help the dickbrain. Perhaps he has been annoying them as well.

'Fuck it, let's get into 'em,' I say, and we charge. The rest of the Chelsea see the movement and surge forward, splitting the thin blue line. Sunderland scurry away under the barriers and down the terrace. The police regroup and we are contained again. There are still five minutes to go and the ground is emptying. Sunderland supporters are leaving all four sides of the stadium. It's not as if they are losing – they are 2–1 up! Then we look down at the car park and see a massive mob gathering.

'What's going on?' I ask the copper standing beside me.

'Oh, that's normal. They're waiting for you lot to leave, and once you are outside you're on your own. There's no escort.'

He chuckles, reminding me of a proud dad introducing his son who has just scored a hat-trick in the local Sunday football league. We peer down. You've got to say this for them: they keep trying, and keep summoning up new energy and new bodies for a set-to. The sheer numbers down there make us apprehensive.

A young-looking, skinny Chelsea fan climbs on to the crush barrier and begins to deliver an incredible speech. 'Look at 'em,' he shouts, motioning towards the Sunderland contingent. 'Look at 'em – a bunch of fucking wankers. They're nothing, no-hopers, no jobs, no nothing. They live in fucking caves, this lot – can't even speak English.' He has the attention of the crowd, and is raising and lowering his voice for effect. This nutcase must have been practising at Speaker's Corner. 'Let's get out there and kick shit out of them. Show 'em we're Chelsea and proud of it. We ain't scared of them – they're all bum bandits and they ain't even proper Geordies.' Everyone cheers and claps. Someone has just made a name for himself.

The final whistle blows and Chelsea have begun life in the second flight with a defeat. No one cares; we have more important business on our minds. With the words of the mystery speaker ringing in our ears, we make our way down the stairs. At the last raised level we spot Babs. He's already out there, shaping up on his own to the Sunderland mob. You can tell by their faces that they can't work out how to deal with this powerful man with one arm. Babs is at his peak and has no fear. There is something about him – opposition fans just know when they come face to face with him that they are dealing with something serious.

Very quickly more of us are by his side. They are trying to decide whether to steam into us or flee. We decide for them. Straight in we go, and off they trot. Funny tribe, this lot – keep mobbing up for an off but bottle out every time. Why bother? We pass the home end and there are more of them, but still they don't want to know. There's no doubt the Roker boys have been well and truly routed every time on their own patch.

I speak too soon. As we walk down the main road to the station we hit a crossroads, and suddenly the heavens open. It is raining bricks, dustbins and planks of wood, and again we are taken by surprise. We scatter along the alleys that seem to run at the rear of all the terraced houses. Sunderland have successfully split us up for the first time and some Chelsea boys are beginning to go down. Our lot from Mitcham literally bump into Eccles, still calm in his brown suede jacket, and are then joined by Babs and his pals. By chance, anyone who is anyone at Chelsea is here in this tight little mob and the feeling of infallibility is almost tangible. There are a good fifty of us now as we walk back out on to the main road.

There are fucking hundreds waiting for us. Now they are into us big time. The northerners are giving us a pasting, with punches coming so fast and furious and from so close that we cannot raise our arms to retaliate. There is no room to move but we continue to push forward. This is it; we are going to get slaughtered. They are kicking our legs away, trying to make us go down, but we know we have to stay upright.

It doesn't take an Eccles command for us to realise that the strategy we are employing is wrong and requires some revision. An animal instinct kicks in and we back off until we are again in the mouth of the alley we had earlier emerged from. The odds are a little better now, as only about twenty of them at a time can get into the alley. We hold firm and are now giving as good as we are getting. Wave upon wave comes at us but we somehow manage to keep them at bay. Talk about Custer's Last Stand. Finally, just as I am wondering where all this will end, we hear a welcome Chelsea roar from behind the mob. The rest of our boys have regrouped and attacked them from behind. We step out of the alley and our attackers run.

We had all fought like gladiators in the mouth of that alley, and it was because we had done, with no one running and no one going down, that we all survived. I now knew why Babsy and Eccles had established such reputations. They had cajoled, scrapped and commanded every inch of the way, giving confidence to each one of us.

'Great stuff,' smiled Eccles, brushing down his coat and jeans. 'Dozy bastards. Numberswise they should have done us there. Now, if they'd come up the back of the alley too . . .'

Babs was already lunging forward, not wishing to indulge in any post-battle analysis. At every crossroad or alley, the same thing happened – Sunderland mounted an assault and we fought it off. But it was wearing us down and finally the initiative was with the locals. The Old Bill were on top of it too and each running ruck was quickly quelled.

Back at Seaburn station we rushed to board the waiting special to ensure we got a seat. It's a long journey home to stand outside the toilet or sit cross-legged by the doors. Whilst we waited for the police to round up the stragglers, we leant back and reflected on the day's events. Sunderland were game but had little staying power. We had done their pub, run them ragged before the game and battered those that were in our end. They had redeemed themselves on the walk back to the station by giving some of us a caning and repeatedly ambushing us, but the conclusion was a comfortable points win.

The train chugged out of the station. Smash! The windows were coming in all over. A brick landed bang in the middle of the card school that the blokes opposite had just opened up. We all dived for cover under the seats as Sunderland practised their synchronised vandalism from a nearby bridge. 'Put your foot down, driver!' shouted some wag to a background noise of shattering glass. After the onslaught we walked up and down the train and saw that every carriage had at least a couple of windows missing. It was summer but there was a chilly wind and we realised that this was going to be even more uncomfortable than the average homeward trip.

We settled back into the newly air-conditioned carriage and talked again about the day. We dozed and we awoke. Some time into the journey we began to look at one another. Steve Brown from Mitcham was first on the list. Steve had three older brothers and one of us noticed that he was wearing a pullover that used to belong to his older brother Mick.

'That's Mick's jumper, ain't it?' asked Steve's Uncle Bob.

'Yeah, and it was Peter's before that,' anticipated Steve, resignedly accepting that it was his turn for a wind-up and trying to get the inevitable over.

'Well,' Bob grinned, 'it's fourth hand and it's gotta go.'

Steve looked puzzled but we all pounced, wrestled the jumper off him and slung it out of the window. We were all cold but Steve was shivering now. The train began to slow and spluttered to a halt.

'I don't believe it,' I said. 'The driver's stopping to pick up yer family heirloom.' We all laughed. Bob had his head poking out of the window and was peering into the distance. 'We're just outside a place called St Neots,' he informed us.

'Where the fuck is that?'

'I don't know, but there's a pub and some shops down there at the bottom of the embankment.'

We had sat back again, waiting for the train to restart, when the British Transport Police walked down the centre aisle.

'Oh, how nice of you to turn up. Where the fuck were you when this train got turned over?' demanded Tony.

'Probably hiding in the khazis,' muttered someone else.

'Pipe down, pipe down,' said the bigger one as if he was addressing an unruly bunch of infant school kids. 'There is a spot of trouble with the train and we are waiting for a part to arrive with the fitters. Be patient, lads, it won't be long now.'

We'd heard that one before. This was another thing about the specials – they constantly broke down, and you'd be waiting in the middle of nowhere for ages. Whether there really was a mechanical breakdown I'll never know. I can't help thinking they were ruses employed by the police to ensure that the arrival times back in London of the various travelling fans were suitably staggered.

Bobby suggested we jump off and visit the shops below for some grub. At that our lot leapt from the train, slid down the embankment and then clambered over the fence, which was designed to stop people getting in, not out. Last one over was Steve Brown.

'Where ya been, Steve – to get yer jumper?' I teased. I then looked up at the train and saw that the remainder of the passengers, not shy about hijacking a good idea, were bumping down the embankment like a human landslide. We ran across the road and into a chip shop.

'Where did you lot come from?' gasped the open-mouthed owner.

'Sunderland,' was the reply.

Delighted by this sudden and unexpected upturn in his business, the owner urged his wife to get shovelling those chipped potatoes into the deep-fat fryer. He probably wanked over things like this. We gulped the food down and made for the pub next door.

'Time for a pint, I think,' said Bobby, rubbing his belly. In we went. The pub was nearly empty and this small business-man (5ft 2ish) also seemed glad of the extra trade. The publican had even laid on a band for the unappreciative St Neots public and they churned out an old Presley song in the corner of the bar.

'Hark at that shit,' jeered Tony.

'If you can do better, get up there,' I challenged.

Tony liked a dare. He put his drink on the bar, swivelled around and strode meaningfully to the mini stage. He snatched the microphone from the singer and continued with the Elvis number the band were halfway through. By now the pub was heaving, as the rest of the lads, stomachs full with cod and chips, had joined us. We gave Tony a standing ovation and he decided to stay for a second song. The band smiled half-heartedly. Peter hopped on to the stage and joined Tony on drums. The real singer slumped into a seat. We stayed for about an hour and had a real scream. Even the few locals who were there clapped along. Tony came off the stage to rejoin his pint, and he puffed up as he was slapped on the back from all angles.

'That was brilliant, Tone,' I enthused. 'I just love Alvin Stardust.'

Back on the train, our jaws were going nineteen to the dozen, our tongues refuelled with alcohol. The fella who had made the Enoch Powell address earlier in the day walked past our table.

'Fair old speech you gave there, Icky,' said Tony. 'You definitely got everyone going.'

Icky smiled, exchanged pleasantries and walked on.

'Who is that geezer?' I asked Tony.

'That's Hickmott. He's from Kent. He's a crank but he's a good bloke.'

* * *

Later that season we played Sunderland at home. Everyone who had been up at their place and more turned out for the return match. At about 2 p.m. a tube train full of Sunderland emerged into the Fulham Road light. A huge Chelsea firm which seconds earlier had been hanging around the White Hart trying hard not to look like a mob legged them straight back down Fulham Broadway stairs. They didn't reappear until ten minutes later, when they were cocooned by police, dogs and horses. This was an escort and a half, and there was no chance of getting at them out on the road now. My girlfriend Mandy was curious to know why we were all so mad keen to get at this lot. I filled her in on the details of our Roker Park visit: the ambushes, the battle at the top of the alley and the wrecked train. I told her about the arsehole with the teeth missing and the bare chest, hanging off the barriers like some old beer-gutted orang-utan and bashing whoever he could reach.

Chelsea wanted a bit of revenge, but our police, unlike their northern counterparts, were intent on protecting the visitors. Our firm decided to nip into the ground – the North Stand end – where the Sunderland would finish up if they made it. Dozens of other firms had the same idea and hundreds of us stood expectantly at the top of the terraces, looking down the hill which led on to the steep concrete steps which Sunderland would soon be climbing. There was barely a policeman in sight, most of them having been deployed on escort duty. Chelsea police were pretty well clued up in most ways but they never seemed to get the hang of the North Stand. Week in, week out, Chelsea got in there to launch the opposing fans. As hard as they tried, they couldn't stop it. We could tell a non-Chelsea fan a mile off, whether they wore colours or not. But in those days the police couldn't. Of course, we didn't arrive as an army and we gained entry singly or in pairs, so it wasn't easy.

The police were now herding Sunderland up the hill towards the turnstiles. Like lambs to the slaughter. There was a very small Chelsea firm beside them but the police didn't realise. Sunderland gained confidence from the sign 'NORTH STAND: VISITING SUPPORTERS ONLY' and let out their first chant of 'Sun-der-land, Sun-der-land, Sun-der-land!'. They thought they were safe and sound and the nightmare was over. Wrong! It had only just begun.

They were about five hundred strong – not a bad turnout for visitors to us – and they squeezed through the turnstiles and began scrambling up the hill to the open terrace. The little firm which had been loitering beside them broke into a run and panicked them up the hill straight into our main mob. We mowed them down like skittles as the little firm picked them off at the rear. They panicked more, shitting it, running one way and then back. No police and heavily outnumbered. Then they stopped dead in their tracks. Some were physically shaking but we tore into them. Some quick-thinking ones attempted to mingle in with us and lose their identity; other silly bastards ran back towards the turnstiles but were systematically taken out and kicked senseless.

Too soon for us but too late for most of them, the police swept in, made a few arrests, lobbed out known troublemakers and swiftly restored order. The remaining Sunderland, now severely chastened, were gathered together and put behind the goal. Some of the northerners amongst us dropped their façade and dashed for the police protection. There seemed to be only around two hundred of them now and it was obvious they had no intention of putting up any sort of fight.

A funny thing about the segregation in the North Stand was that at half-time both sets of fans were allowed to queue for their drinks and food at the same burger stalls. So much for the security of the visitors. Mandy and I joined the long line which snaked down the terraces. God knows why. The tea was always cold, the Bovril was so thick you could have fixed a roof leak with it and the burgers and hot dogs defied description. In front of us we could hear two northern accents clucking quietly.

'How the fuck are we going to get out of here?' asked one.

'Fuck knows,' replied the other, shaking his head. 'If the coppers don't keep us behind, we'll get massacred.'

They shuffled forwards, glancing furtively around like pilots who have baled out behind enemy lines. If they were that worried they should have passed on the half-time nosh, but with our friends in the north there is little that competes with the urge to eat. One of them, hearing Mandy's voice, looked around and half smiled. He was trying to make contact with her femininity, something soft in a cauldron of hate. But, you see, he shouldn't have done that, because as he smiled he revealed a severe absence of teeth.

'That's that wanker from up in Sunderland,' I whispered. 'The one with most of his railings missing. He's got some neck coming down here. He's either got a lot of arsehole or he's plain fucking stupid.'

They bought their tea and burgers and began to walk along the back of the terraces to rejoin the rest of their party. Unfortunately for them, they'd already been spotted by other eagle-eyed Chelsea boys.

'Hello, big mouth,' announced one Chelsea fan, standing square in front of him and blocking his path. Whack! The Chelsea boy's fist plunged straight into his face. He dropped his drink and burger – which probably added to his pain – and tried to make a run for it. In seconds both men were completely surrounded. Icky had noticed the commotion and also recognised the tooth fairy.

'Let's see you get out of this one,' he laughed. 'You're not so fucking mouthy now.'

The Sunderland mateys stood frozen to the spot. They looked at the ground so as not to engage anyone's stare. They reminded me of Vietnamese peasants awaiting the American bullet in the side of the head.

'It's pay-back time,' said Icky again in a mock posh voice, but the cavalry appeared in the shape of the Met and bundled the Sunderland Two to the relative safety of their pals. Mandy and I followed and positioned ourselves behind them.

'What happened to you?' asked one of his mates. 'You've got blood coming out yer hooter.'

'I got ambushed by Chelsea,' he explained. 'There's hundreds of them up the top.'

I tapped him on the shoulder and he looked around.

'Remember me?'

'No, should I?' he sniffed cautiously.

'Well, you see, I'm a Chelsea fan and I went up to your place back in August and, if you remember, you made yourself a bit busy. Didn't you?' His face was dropping by the second, like he had had a stroke. 'There are a lot of people here who would like to shake you firmly by the throat.'

'How do you know it's me?' Clutching at straws now.

'It's yer teeth, or should I say lack of them, and within an hour any you've got left will be going AWOL too.'

He swallowed hard, wiping his face with the back of his hand and leaving a blood stain across his cheek like a brush stroke. I hadn't hit him yet. I was with a bird. He tried to appeal to my better nature.

'Can you help me out?' he pleaded.

'No chance, and whoever is with you is going to cop it as well.'

I continued to wind him up for the rest of the match, telling him every five minutes how long there was left to the end of the game. At the final whistle we all made our way along the back of the terrace to the only exit. Chelsea were now openly mingling with Sunderland.

'Come on, mate, help me out, please. I didn't mean anything back home. I was only joking.'

I was his mate now, it seemed.

'Don't worry, the Chelsea boys are only joking too.'

I smiled as menacingly as I could, relishing his anguish. Around him his fellow travellers were being picked off at random and getting kicked all the way down the mud bank that led to the railway sidings. He moved closer to me and Mandy. Eventually we went out on to the road and he turned right towards the tube. Malice hung heavily in the air, along with the stench of horse shit and hot-dog fumes. Horses trotted in every direction, dispersing dozens of guerrilla attacks on the traumatised Sunderland fans. My best mate's Adam's apple was bouncing around his neck like a ping-pong ball as he neared the station. Every now and then I leant towards him and smiled, and I swear his eyes were watering. Finally we hit the station entrance. He was safe unless Icky and the boys were planning an Earls Court ambush for the travelling fans. I touched his arm and he looked at me fearfully.

'Be lucky. Safe journey.'

He nodded, still unsure as to what might happen next.

'By the way,' I shouted as I stepped towards the White Hart, 'wrap yerself up!'

SEVEN

Life in the Lower Leagues

When a small-town club from the lower divisions are playing a big team who have been relegated, and that team are from London and have a history of troublesome followers, then fireworks and fisticuffs are very much on the cards. The locals feel duty-bound to put up some sort of a show against the invading forces. An occupying army is in town – at best they must be repelled and defeated; at worst they must be subjected to various acts of sabotage or some show of resistance. Followers of Manchester United, Spurs, Leeds and Newcastle, all of whom have dropped into the pits of the Second Division at some point, will all testify to having been confronted by seething mobs in places they least expected it. Whole communities have been known to turn out. Not just the football thugs, but Hell's Angels, left-wing groups, the Women's Institute and the town's morris-dancing troop. Chelsea's stint in the lower division was no exception.

What was different was the way that Chelsea's excursions were always accompanied by a media circus. Reporters and photographers had it in their heads that Chelsea were the team to follow for guaranteed trouble. It became self-perpetuating: trouble at Chelsea, media creates monster, Chelsea becomes monster to live up to media creation. Every week in the mid '70s, pictures and reports of fighting were plastered across the papers, more often than not involving Chelsea fans. But then Chelsea always seem to attract disproportionate interest, both on and off the field. President Clinton even named his daughter after his favourite English mob.

But there was trouble all over Britain at this time. It was the fashion. Most young men from the working and not-working classes aligned themselves with a club and for varying periods of time would get involved in rucking with other supporters. The 'minority' that the press always referred to was bollocks. Millwall v. Chelsea; gate –11,000. I'd bet my life that at least half that crowd, and more likely three-quarters, were there for the knuckle. The percentage may not have been so high at other games, but minority it was not.

The media liked following Chelsea, though. It was sexier to report 'rioting' involving Chelsea fans than a pitched battle between, say, Reading and Oxford fans. Like other fashions, as a hobby for the masses, hooliganism went in and went out. When it was out, a hard core of committed and experienced supporters were left eager to defend their team and their firm's good name.

The few seasons that the Blues wallowed in the old Second Division, I went to most away games, some of them being among the most memorable in all the time I have followed the team. At Plymouth the whole town turned out, along with the navy, but we had an idea what to expect. The hooligan grapevine was always alive with information. Saturday's fights, victories and defeats were generally known by other mobs by the following week, the stories filtering across the divides. Tottenham got run by Leeds, Man City turned over Newcastle's pub and so on. Plymouth had played Everton in the FA Cup a couple of weeks earlier and we had heard that the scousers had taken quite a caning.

The train arrived at Plymouth station and there was the customary rush to get off the platform and out on to the street. There was a pub opposite but a quick peek inside showed no boys in there. We carried on into a park which contained their stadium, hence the name of the ground, Home Park. There was an hour to go before kick-off, we had no police escort and we were all playing around the recreation ground like a load of oversized kids. Walking past the visiting supporters' end, we were spotted by the thousands of Chelsea already in there. A chorus of 'Que será, será, whatever will be, will be, we're going to Wem-ber-lee' went up. This wasn't even a cup match but the Chelsea scarves and hats seemed to like singing that one.

We joined the Plymouth fans queuing to enter the home end. They knew who we were. We didn't have to talk; the clothes gave it away. We could have just stepped off the set of *Saturday Night Fever* in our capped-sleeved T-shirts, blowing in the cold sea wind, and our high-waistband trousers with two belts. Yes, two ridiculous thin belts. They, on the other hand, looked like they had been ploughing the fields or had just stepped off a fishing trawler, with their donkey jackets, bobble hats, army trousers and hob-nailed boots. And that was just the girls – the men didn't dress any smarter.

Inside the ground we gathered behind the goal. There were about two hundred of us. At the other end, Chelsea were in full song – 'When Butch goes up, to lift the FA Cup, we'll be there, we'll be there' – still oblivious, it seemed, to the fact that this was a pedestrian league game, not a cup-tie. The West Country boys gathered discreetly around us. They were spaced out, quiet and didn't appear threatening in any way. More poured in from outside. Word must have got around that cockneys were taking liberties and were in Plymouth's end. The teams ran on to the pitch and, regardless of our situation, we gave Chelsea a rousing reception – and this was the signal for the attack. They piled down the terrace at us, but we ran upwards towards them. They paused and so did we. The usual no-man's land opened up and it was a stand-off. The no-man's land was useful inasmuch as it gave the side that would eventually run a head start. Our reputation was obviously going before us because we were outnumbered by at least five to one but still they were not sure.

Then, as was often the case, the local herbert stepped forward. There was always one. Normally a fat-gutted lump who had trouble keeping his dirty jeans above his waist, with tattoos on his eyelids and an egg for a brain. The idea was to make a name for himself, to go down in local folklore as the hero who single-handedly took on the fearsome, right-wing,

Hitler-loving, jellied-eel-munching Chelsea army. Today was to be no different, because out of their mob emerged a twenty-stone beer monster with a long beard and greasy, shoulder-length hair. I think he might have been beamed in from grizzly-bear country. He even wore dungarees with no shirt, the folds of his giant belly hanging out from both sides. A real swamp man. He tossed his hair out of his eyes like a lion shaking its mane and walked across towards us. I don't know if he went down in Plymouth folklore but he certainly went down. A swift kick in the nuts followed by a well-planted uppercut saw to that.

On seeing Goliath writhing on the floor clutching his balls, our Plymouth opponents stepped back and back and back. We ran them over to the corner of the end, trampling over Grizzly Adams in the process. They jumped the small wall that surrounded the pitch, with the game still going on. The police came charging in to restore order. They led us across the terrace with the intention of putting us in our rightful end with the other visitors from London. There were about twenty of us lagging behind the main escort, relaxed and laughing about the lack of serious opposition. Another Plymouth lot had identified this opportunity to have a pop at us stragglers and they struck quickly. A few of us took some vicious blows but we managed to turn and face the attack and hit back. This time, though, they were not backing down. I think these were their top boys, and they meant business.

The police had continued up the terrace, ignoring the fracas. They were more concerned, it seemed, with removing the bulk of the Chelsea contingent from the end. The row was toe to toe and went on for a good couple of minutes, but all the time their numbers were increasing. We backed off and went under the metal crush barrier, which gave us a lull in the action. I took two backwards paces to allow myself some room in which to fight and pick them off as they came under. Then there was an almighty shove from behind and we all went tumbling into the enemy. Bastards! They had sneaked behind us too and now we were trapped. The pressure that had forced us into the front line continued and we were propelled deep into their throng.

It soon became apparent, though, that it was Chelsea bearing down on us, not Plymouth; they had seen our predicament, broken through the police rank and returned to rescue us. Good job, too; things had not been looking too promising. Again the Devonians found themselves fleeing in their own end, and we allowed ourselves to be led out by the police to the opposite end of the ground.

'They're a bit fucking tasty,' said my mate Bobby, blowing out air when we were back with the masses. Bob had been taking the worst of the punishment along with me and a few others.

'They'll be up for it after,' said Tony. 'Best keep our little mob together.'

About twenty of us from Mitcham always tried to stick together and look out for one another. There were legions of Chelsea at the time and loads of faces, but it was always the best policy to keep with the firm you knew. The people you lived with, drank with and worked with. Bottling was not an option.

We'd been to Luton a few weeks earlier and the town had been trashed by a crowd bent on destruction. A Pakistani shopkeeper who had tried to protect his shop had been lassoed with a rope and tied to his door handle. The boys then lined up to pelt him with fruit from his own store. Across the road was a mosque, and on hearing the screams of their fellow countryman all the menfolk from the mosque poured out on to the street. The Chelsea fruit squad looked over, threw a few consolation plums in the general direction of the mosque and before our very eyes disappeared into thin air. This left us Mitcham boys facing up to around fifty or so Asians who appeared very, very angry. Had we shown any fear we would have been in trouble. Without any verbal communication, we all knew what we had to do. We grabbed some metal dustbin lids from outside the shop and ran across the road, forcing the Pakistanis back into the mosque. A couple of blokes who had watched the rumpus said it had reminded them of an Anglo-Saxon army repelling Asian invaders.

At the end of the Plymouth game we decided to hang

around and let the Chelsea scarves and hanger-on hooligans disperse back to the station, and then have a sniff around for some action. Eccles had taken a posse off ten minutes before the final whistle to wait outside the home end. This was a favourite ploy of his. The element of surprise, I suppose. As we leant on the barrier, allowing the Chelsea to push and shove their way out, we saw the Plymouth fans come galloping back into their end, hotly pursued by the Eccles snatch squad. You can always tell at a distance whether a running mob is chasing or being chased. Chasers run grouped together. The chased split up and run in different directions. An appreciative roar rang out, followed by a round of applause and exaggerated laughing as the departing Chelsea fans delighted in Plymouth's humiliation.

We arrived at the other end of the ground just as the Chelsea firm that had been doing the chasing were coming back out. Icky bounced towards us with his big toothy grin and bog-brush haircut. He told us how they had just strolled into the end when the gates opened at full-time and Plymouth had just freaked, running off in a complete panic. As he talked, in between laughs, he looked over our heads, behind himself and sideways. He was anxious he might be missing out on more fun and games. Icky was becoming well known at Chelsea by then; he was constantly laughing and joking, putting on silly voices and making impromptu speeches. At Orient he had turned up in a full gorilla suit and got himself filmed on TV's *The Big Match*. Little did anyone know that the press would one day transform him into a deranged anarchist who threatened the very fabric of society.

Looking back, the policing that day was unbelievable. No escort from the train, no attempts at segregation and a mob of Chelsea allowed to roam in and out of the ground at their leisure. It was surreal, really. Everyone knew where and when we were coming. By now it was common knowledge that Chelsea had a crack at every opposing end, so you didn't need to be Einstein to work out that there was going to be trouble. As usual, the blame was put firmly at the door of Chelsea Football Club, which was unfair. The club can only attempt to ban known troublemakers; they can't be expected to do the other club's policing for them. Chelsea FC carried the can for us followers over the years, which was a bit short-sighted. We were not on the pay-roll, we were not sponsored and most of us were not invited. CFC were about as responsible for us as Whitbread were for lager louts or Ford for joy-riders.

Unlike at Plymouth, the Old Bill at Cardiff were very visible, organised and efficient. They were also very fair: if you were collared you were nicked, whether you were Chelsea or Cardiff. They had us off the train and into the ground in a jiffy. We were placed in an enclosure along the side of the pitch, not behind the goal as at most games. There were Welsh nutters all over but the police had them on a tight leash. Cardiff fans are well up for a row, always have been. Man United and Spurs have both come unstuck against the Taffies, and even our friends at Millwall have a healthy respect for them. Millwall were always starved of action at home on account of the fact that most lower-league clubs are either too frightened to visit or don't have any away support. Cardiff were one of the few that livened up proceedings at the Den.

Although the police had sewn up us boys from the train, they were less successful with the many hundreds who had come up on coaches. Hickmott was by now operating 'Icky's Luxury Coaches' and he led his merry men straight into the Cardiff end, which, curiously, was situated directly opposite us. Flamboyant as ever, Icky unfolded a St George's Cross flag for all to see. This was like a red rag to a bull, and the Taffs went apeshit. They flew into the coachload with a viciousness that made those of us watching from the other side of the pitch cringe. Compared to Plymouth, for example, Cardiff were a different class. They got in between Chelsea, splitting them up and then mercilessly kicking fuck out of those who fell. It was every man for himself and we could only watch and cheer on our boys. It was obvious that they were copping a hiding.

The fighting had spread from the centre of the end right up to the far side, just above the corner flag. Here a small bunch of Chelsea had managed to compose themselves and were giving a good account, even driving Cardiff back a bit. Slowly, though, the sheer force of numbers pushed them up to the top of the concrete steps.

'They've done well to stay in there this long,' I commented to my mate Brian Wilkes.

'There's only about fifty left, by the looks of it,' he observed.

I doubt if many teams venture into the middle of the Cardiff lot and come out in one piece. Swivelling our heads around, we saw that a scuffle had broken out again in the middle of the end. We could clearly see one solitary man tearing into the Cardiff fans. His arms and legs were going like a windmill as he knocked down the Taffies as they came at him, one after another. The Welsh kept jumping on his back and he managed to throw each of them off, holding the rest at bay with his arms and legs. I was reminded of the Incredible Hulk. He kept this up for a couple of minutes – which is a long time when you're scrapping for your life – but finally disappeared under a sea of bodies. This had been some battling performance from the unknown fruitcake.

Just as we were lamenting his fate, the crowd parted and backed away. We couldn't see, but thought, has he pulled a knife? A gun? We found out later that the Cardiff boys had decided he'd taken enough punishment and allowed him back to his feet. See, there is honour among football thugs! As soon as he was upright, though, he started planting everyone around him again and they motored back into him. The police finally broke through the crowd and removed the man from the terrace. As they hoisted him over the wall and on to the pitch, where they began to lead him off, a sincere round of applause rang out from the Cardiff fans. It was unbelievable. They were saluting this lone warrior as if he was a young boxer who had just gone twelve rounds with a tough old pro. Who said that sportsmanship has gone out of football?

The police treated him fairly and with respect and put him over with us. He got a hero's reception. It was Melvyn. One of Hickmott's motley crew, he was a former Southampton fan who had changed his allegiance to Chelsea because, as he said, you were guaranteed a better row at Chelsea. Melvyn certainly had a better row that day.

Icky himself had by now been transferred into our enclosure. He stood next to Melvyn.

'I think we did rather well out there,' he drawled. 'Not many come out of there laughing.'

That was it for him. One big giggle.

Just before the end of the game, a small group of Cardiff fans, about thirty strong, gathered below us at the foot of the steps at the exit from our end. One of them at the front was giving us a lot of trap. He had long hair, parted at the side, a flowery shirt and a lairy pair of flared trousers. He was a ringer for little Jimmy Osmond.

'Fuck off, you little Welsh prick, and go shag your sister, Marie,' we taunted, but it seemed to go over his head.

'Wait till you get out here, you flash cockney bastards! We'll show you what it's all about,' he snarled up at us.

At that we broke out into the chorus of 'Long-Haired Lover from Liverpool', which completely threw him. At the same time a few of the lads vaulted the small wall where we stood and dropped the ten feet or so straight into the middle of the Taffs. The Welsh branch of the extended Osmond family froze to the spot as all the other Chelsea fans in the end threw themselves over the wall. Chelsea were pouring down on them like hailstones, and after a few kicks up the arse the Cardiff crew ran off. The police were equally nonplussed, as the end was emptying but they hadn't seen anyone leave.

Outside, the Cardiff lot who had been goading us were now standing in a park inviting us in. There were about three hundred Welsh standing in there. We climbed the four-foot metal railings and landed in the park. We walked towards them and they walked towards us. It was like *Gunfight at the OK Corral.* Even numbers and both sides wondering whose nerve was going to go first. I looked around and had the comfort of seeing all the faces I knew. There were the Mitcham boys, there was Hickmott, there was Melvyn, with his shirt hanging on him in shreds, and there were a couple of hundred others. No fear. We might get beaten but we were not going to run. At this time, this was happening every other week. Run of the mill.

The Taffs stopped about fifty feet from us and the front line turned and ran. Or tried to. The ones behind continued to push forward; after all, it wasn't them who were going to take the first flurry of blows. They trod on each other and fell over each other as panic spread like a forest fire among them – and we hadn't gone into them yet. We did, though, and the ones who got caught took a real battering. The police soon intervened and managed to shepherd us back on to our trains.

At Newport station the train was in and the platform was alive with police and dogs. For an hour nothing seemed to be happening. We leant out of the window and chatted with the Welsh Old Bill, who, unlike most other forces, were friendly and relaxed. They informed us that they were waiting for their plain-clothes colleagues to arrive from Cardiff. Apparently a couple of Cardiff fans had been stabbed and in the rush to remove us from their manor they thought they had put the culprit on the train. The CID duly arrived and, carriage by carriage, we were told to stand on the platform and were looked up and down. Not searched, though. It was still a bit nerve-wracking, as you never know when you might get fitted up.

To my knowledge, no one was chivvied in the park that day. I never heard a Chelsea fan claim responsibility either then or later. No one was nicked and we were allowed to continue our journey home. A rumour flashed up and down the train that it was Swansea fans, Cardiff's arch enemies, who were responsible, but no more was heard and there was nothing at all about it in the papers the next day. Had there really been two serious stabbings, you would have thought it would have made the news, but it didn't. This was often the case: incidents that you thought would hit the headlines never did, but you would read about riots at games you'd attended that certainly had not taken place.

* * *

The Second Division game that caught the imagination of most Chelsea fans was the clash against Millwall at the Den. No one cared about the result on the pitch; both teams were pretty uninspiring at the time. It was how the supporters would perform inside and outside the ground that dominated conversation for weeks. Anticipation was so high that some chantmaster even made up a song that they were singing at Chelsea for ages before the actual fixture. It was lifted from a record out at the time about a fight between Muhammad Ali and Joe Frazier, and it went: 'Once there was a battle there/In Mill, in Millwall/Twelve thousand Chelsea there/In Mill, in Millwall/Who was the victor on the night?' and so on.

Both sets of fans had a fearsome reputation but Millwall had the edge when it came to rowing. They couldn't muster the numbers of Chelsea, West Ham or Spurs but they more than made up for it in front. If West Ham were the Kray twins of football thuggery and Chelsea were the Richardsons, Millwall were Frankie Fraser. Mad, bad and dangerous. Their fan base was Peckham, Bermondsey, Deptford, Lewisham and the surrounding areas. Millwall chaps all had a certain swagger and confidence about them. West Ham boys were the same. They were under the impression that because their clubs were associated with the docks, they were all eight foot tall, weighed twenty-five stone and had gone the distance with Alan Minter. A load of bollocks, really. As accurate as the belief that all Chelsea fans were pink-shirted nancies who drove up and down the King's Road in open-topped MGBs. Millwall revelled in the image, though. The ground was even called the Den! The area was drab and depressing and the reputation of the club was one of the few things that the community was really proud of. Perverse as it may seem, the older folk and the non-football fans of the area could often be seen clapping and cheering as their boys dished out a good spanking to anyone foolhardy enough to turn up at the New Cross stations.

But Chelsea were on a roll. Our reputation was on the up again. We had been turning over every Second Division ground we visited and the papers, at least, thought we were the ones to fear. Publicly we feared no one, but privately Millwall was about the only club we were not sure we were ready for. We knew a lot was at stake and it almost made your eyes water when you saw the faces that came out of the woodwork for this one. Eccles had arranged a meet at 11 a.m. at Fulham Broadway and I spied people I had not seen for seven or eight years, excitedly banging their rolled-up copies of the *Sun* against their thighs. Men in their mid-thirties, some of them, and we were going to need them, I remember thinking. Babsy had a separate rendezvous at the Bull pub in Lewisham. The Eccles meet was, as usual, a bit on the early side, but that was him all over. In the event we hung around Fulham until around midday, as the General was keen to ensure we had as many top faces as possible and there seemed to be a few people he was reluctant to leave without. Eventually we took the District Line to Whitechapel and changed, catching the East London Line to Surrey Docks, where we alighted. We came out on to the streets, three hundred of us, and the place was deserted except for an old man standing outside a battered old newsagent, peering over at us.

'Across the park,' someone shouted. A couple of minutes later, 'Back out on the road.'

This is a good start, I thought. Eccles pushed his way to the front, clutching an A–Z of London. He loved a map. Studying it for a minute with furrowed brow, he muttered almost to himself, 'Park on our left.' He looked over and confirmed that the park was indeed still on our left. He turned the book upside down.

'Right up here, then we do a left and then a right. Then we'll hit one of their boozers, but we gotta sneak past this. We don't really want to have it here this early. We need to meet up with Babs and then go for the main event.'

We followed obediently, and as we approached the pub he stopped and motioned for us all to crouch down and walk almost on all fours past the large bay windows.

'Quiet!' he commanded.

I looked at Peter Stevens and he looked at me. Was this bloke serious?

'Hang on,' I ventured. 'Isn't this why we are here? To have a ruck with Millwall? Not to get down on our knees and crawl past their pubs!'

He shot me the exasperated look that you would get from a

teacher when you interrupted their flow by putting your hand up in class and asking an inane question.

'Who's running this show?'

So down we got. Three hundred Chelsea yobs crouched low and passed beneath the window ledges of the pub in dead silence. What a sight it must have been to any passers-by or residents. Bollocks, I thought, as I passed the second window. I stood bolt upright and looked straight in. The pub was empty save one toothless old git nursing half a brown ale and sucking on a roll-up.

We soon reached the tunnels which led behind the Cold Blow Lane end of the ground, which is where the home fans stand – although the term 'home fans' is a bit of a misnomer at Millwall, as there are very rarely any away fans. Millwall stand wherever they want. We began to queue to get into the ground. I spotted a small group of Millwall fans just the other side of the gate. They did not seem at all perturbed about our numbers. They had that 'we know something you don't' look about them. They screwed at us and us at them. Apart from a couple of small clusters of people, the ground was empty, and we moved to the top centre of the end. The atmosphere was heavy and forbidding. The calm before the storm. No one spoke but I'm sure we were all thinking the same thing: why the fuck had we come in here? Making a show at Millwall in our heavily policed designated end would have been sufficient to hold our heads up. Camping out in their main end was really going for the big one.

Word must have got around that we were in there because one minute the ground was empty and the next people were pouring in from every entrance. The alarming thing was that from wherever in the ground they were appearing, they were heading straight towards the Cold Blow Lane end and most probably us. We hadn't roared up or anything but there was no doubt who we were. Fifty or so Millwall boys had soon gathered below us on the terrace and more of their mob were very quickly on both sides. The Old Bill just stood around chatting to one another, ignoring the posturing and position-ing that was taking place. Perhaps they too were locals and were happy for us to be taught a lesson for our audacity. Arseholes among the Chelsea boys began to twitch and quite a few of our number slipped themselves into the Millwall crowd, trying to blend in and save their skins. Others were more open and walked rapidly down the stairs, climbed over the turnstile and went back into the street from where they had jauntily entered only fifteen minutes earlier.

Without a punch being thrown or a threat made, Millwall had successfully managed to psyche a lot of the Chelsea boys out. There had been no trouble yet and we were already down to around a hundred, surrounded by the nastiest mob I had come across yet. A fight broke out behind us; Millwall had come up the stairs from the forecourt below and steamed in from behind. At this they came at us from both sides. We did well, the guys at the back turning and facing the rear attack, the blokes at the side trading off with the attack from the flanks and us lot concentrating on the Millwall firm in front of us. We held off their first real assault and they seemed a touch surprised.

A big black geezer with horn-rimmed glasses was making it his job to dig me out.

'Oi, white boy! Leave now or you're going to die.'

'Fuck off, you silly black tosser,' I retorted. 'Keep on and you'll be the one dying.'

I didn't give a fuck about the Old Kent Road swagger and bravado. I had my own. Didn't give a shit for anyone – it was the Romany blood in me. What did he think I was going to say? 'Sorry old boy, I'll just be off. Thanks.' Bow, scrape. Bollocks.

'Come on, just me and you.'

He motioned me down the terrace towards him. I could see he didn't fancy coming up the steps and ducking under the barrier to me.

'Do him!' urged his mates.

'Come on, fat boy! Wobble up here and let me give you a lesson in respect.'

'Do him!' shouted the Millwall. 'Don't let these Chelsea wankers take the piss.'

With that he swung himself under the barrier. I moved down a step or two and cracked him straight on the jaw. His body went one way and his glasses the other. The rest of the Millwall scattered down the terrace, many jumping the fence and going out on to the pitch. We were well pleased: it was getting near kick-off and we were still in the end, holding off attacks from all angles and having just run a group of them on to the pitch. But we knew this was just the beginning.

The Den was a strange ground. You could walk all the way round, it seemed. And it seemed like every single member of that crowd was being drawn towards our little group, as one. A huge Millwall fan, all brawn and no fat and at least forty years old, stepped out in front of us.

'Come on, Chelsea, who wants it?'

I bet he was a bouncer from one of the pubs on the Old Kent Road. He's a bit big for me, I thought. I'd have to catch him right to knock him out. I'll leave him for someone else. Someone else duly stepped from among us and lamped this geezer straight on the jaw. His fist bounced off. Desperate Dan didn't move an inch.

More of our mob evaporated into the crowd. I call this melting. This day it was meltdown, and we were down to about fifty now. All over the ground, short scuffles were taking place as Millwall systematically rooted out small pockets of Chelsea and turned them over. As the last group of Chelsea obviously together, we became even more the focus of their attention. We had a thin line of police protecting us from a full-scale assault, but it was scant comfort. This lot could overpower the police presence around us any time they wanted.

'Martin, Martin, over here!'

It was my mate Peter Stevens, who was on the Millwall side of the police line. He was with Dave Perks, the Chelsea fan who had defected to West Ham. They both urged me to come and stand with them.

'I'm with some of Millwall's main faces,' reassured Perks.

'Big fucking deal. I'm with Chelsea's main faces,' I responded, 'and what's a West Ham boy doing here anyway?'

He looked straight ahead in an effort to make out that the last comment had not been directed at him.

By now my mate, the black man with the glasses, was back. He wasn't so mouthy this time but stood staring at me. He was trying to put over the message that he was past shouting. This was the judgement hour. He was trying to stare into my soul and convince me I was about to die. It was an act for the benefit of his followers. He had lost face as well as his spectacles. He could have picked up a Best Actor Oscar, his performance was that good. The problem was, I couldn't get out of my mind the image of his glasses flying across the terrace when I whacked him.

The team came out and the Millwall came in. A second's diversion and they attacked from all sides; the police were lost somewhere in the middle. We found ourselves in the far corner of the end, not only fighting for Chelsea but fighting for our lives. So many of them were trying to hammer us at the same time, very few were succeeding. If they had contained their frenzy and taken it a bit more slowly, I think we might have died. Really. Some police, visibly shocked by the ferocity that had been unleashed, bundled us down some steps that led to the forecourt. When I say us, I could see now it was actually only two of us. Me and Bernie Marsh, a Chelsea boy from Crawley. I know now how the Welsh Guard must have felt at Rorke's Drift.

A burly policeman let us out through the gates with a shove. 'You've had yer fun, now fuck off out of it.'

Fun? Are you sure? Bernie and I faced one another, hearts pounding. I didn't waste any time and walked back to the Elephant and Castle, where I got the tube back to my girl-friend's house. Back to normality and safety. Away from that hell hole. I knew there would be no show afterwards and that the streets of Deptford would be no place for chastened Chelsea fans.

I learned later that as we had been running the gauntlet on the way out of the Cold Blow Lane end, Babs and his mob had been coming in. Babs had adopted the opposite strategy to Eccles by getting in late and surprising the Millwall fans.

Apparently they did quite well and lasted until ten minutes from the end, when, as with our lot, some serious melting took place and they too were literally pummelled out of the ground.

Our two mobs got off lightly in some respects. The real story of the afternoon was the savage beatings dished out to Chelsea fans, in twos, threes and fours, who tried to make their way back to trains and cars in the dank south London backstreets. Everyone had a story. Only a few Chelsea boys who turned up that day can say they came away completely unscathed. Colin Daniels tells a story that is typical of the goings-on that late afternoon. He was with a group of five or six and they had successfully negotiated a web of unfamiliar backstreets to avoid the worst of the fighting and the ambushes. They felt they were heading in the general direction of the Elephant. As they walked slightly less hurriedly, a rag-and-bone man with his horse and cart trotted towards them. As the cart drew level, a bunch of Millwall jumped up, throwing off the sacking they had been hiding under. The first one off leapt at Colin and smashed a china vase straight over his head.

Over the years, I have heard how the true stories of that day have been turned into fairytales. One I am told from time to time by Millwall fans is that they ripped off Babs's false arm and threw it on to the pitch. In all the years I knew Babsy, I never saw him wear such a thing.

We were routed that day but on the whole I don't think we did too badly. No one in those days – and that means *no one* – ever took the fight to Millwall, but we did. Not only did we turn up, but we went in their end. Twice. Two different mobs. For a long time we held our own. It made us pause for thought, though. I think it made us organise ourselves a bit better. After that we were less tolerant of melters. We made it clear there was no room with us if you were going to melt. Mainly, though, we had met a bogeyman head on, and after that there was nothing to be scared of.

I think even Millwall had a respect for us after that afternoon. We have played them many times since and there is normally serious trouble, but of all the clubs, I think Chelsea and Millwall enjoy a special relationship. I've been to many games involving Millwall and have the highest regard for their boys; a lot of them know I'm Chelsea but they give me no grief. There are Millwall connections with a few other firms at Chelsea too. Seeing that that game in the mid '70s was the first time for years that the two sets of fans had come into contact with one other, I suspect that the (mostly) cordial relations stem from that day.

EIGHT

Amateur Football, Professional Fights

We were all huddled around a cement-stained transistor radio on a building site in Mitcham. What was this momentous event? The Queen's speech? A president assassinated? No, it was far more important. We were awaiting the draw for the third round of the FA Cup. Our little local club Tooting and Mitcham, who played in the Surrey Cherrypickers League or something, were in the hat with the First Division big boys. The draw was always live on the radio in those days before overweight Football Association clerks became convinced they were celebrities too and stuck themselves in front of every passing camera. 'Tooting and Mitcham will play . . . Crystal Palace,' announced the plummy FA voice. We all roared up, punching the air. The consensus was that it would go right off. Palace were just down the road, so the ingredients were in place for a local derby with all the passion of a Chelsea–Spurs or a Millwall–West Ham.

Now, Palace were always a funny club. On geographical grounds we Mitcham boys should have supported them, but few of us did. Selhurst Park was within gobbing distance of some really hard areas but they never had much of a mob, and although their gates were healthy, the fans did not seem to have much fervour. They seemed to take the piss out of themselves, from the ritual singing of the Dave Clark Five's 'Glad All Over' before matches to their ridiculous and monotonous 'Eagles' chant. For a long while they even had a manager called Bert (Knob) Head. They constantly hovered around the bottom of the First Division despite having some talented players like Don Rogers, who resembled a Mexican bandit sprinting down the wing, and stocky Peter Taylor. In addition there was a trickle of old Chelsea players put out to grass there, such as Charlie Cooke, Bobby Tambling and Alan Birchenall. There was rarely trouble, at least when Chelsea played them. Unlike other clubs, they didn't even put up a pretence of having a go at the likes of us or West Ham, Arsenal or Tottenham, but they could raise a few herberts for the lesser fixtures. The annual match against Brighton, for example, nearly always ended in a battle between the two sets of supporters, Eagles and Seagulls pecking each other's eyes out.

Due to some technical problem with Tooting's floodlights – like they didn't work – the match was to be played on a Wednesday afternoon at 2 p.m. rather than the traditional Saturday at 3 p.m. All of us on the site decided that we would knock off early on that Wednesday and go and support our local side. I say 'local', but working on that site were followers of Chelsea, Man U, Millwall, Spurs, Rangers, Celtic – you name it. There was the usual Irish contingent too (it was a Wimpey site and we used to jest that Wimpey was an acronym for We Import More Paddies Every Year) who supported teams whose names meant nothing to us, but we were all Tooting and Mitcham for that day.

On the Wednesday in question we left work at midday and headed for our rendezvous – the Nag's Head in the centre of Mitcham. The pub was buzzing with anticipation. It was already jam-packed with males of all ages, as word had spread around the area that all Tooting and Mitcham were coming out to play for this one. A smattering of Chelsea faces were in there sinking the lager, along with a few from other London clubs, but the vast majority were local hard nuts. Hard nuts without the slightest interest in football. The lure of a local ruck had brought them out.

Rumour had it that Palace were coming by bus from Croydon and they were going to march through the town centre on their way to the ground. As with most football punch-up rumours, this turned out to be bullshit and two hundred of us hung around the pub in vain. These rumours were the scourge of our lives: Tottenham are coming down the Black Bull at midday, Arsenal are getting in the Shed early, Millwall and West Ham are meeting at Earls Court at 1 p.m., Everton are drinking in a boozer in Grays Inn Road, and so on. It was all bollocks normally. There was always someone who worked with someone whose brother was a Spurs top boy or whatever. I don't know why we listened to any of them. I suppose it added to the excitement at the time. But there was to be no shortage of excitement on this day.

We set off for the ground and soon an Austin 1100 motor with a little racing steering wheel skidded up alongside us. About seven of our lot from Tooting were squashed into it.

'They're here,' said the driver, barely able to contain his glee. 'About a hundred of them have just come out of Tooting Junction station.'

We quickly made off towards Figgs Marsh, a grassy area between the station and where the Palace crew had just been spotted, only to see the tail end of their mob disappear down Sandy Lane to the ground. We were disappointed because we had the terrain to have a real off and no police were in sight.

It was soon obvious that the Old Bill were treating the fixture with kid gloves. A Category D match, I think the Football (un)Intelligence Unit would term it these days. There were few uniforms to be seen and certainly no horses or dogs. Palace fans, too, shared this low-key approach; the way they were swanning around Mitcham and chanting inside the ground told us this. We pushed into the ground. Most of us did not have tickets but the turnstiles and security were unable to stop us.

Palace had congregated behind the goal at the opposite end, so we eased our way through the crowd to join them. By the time we reached the corner flag they had tumbled. Accompanied by a huge war cry, they charged towards us. Fucking hell, I thought, they think we are the village idiots. They are a First Division club and we are non-league, therefore they are superior. Wrong. They were soon to find we were composed of Cockney Reds, Chelsea, Arsenal, gypsies, prize fighters, minor gangsters, criminals, Irish labourers and Uncle Tom Cobleigh and all. As they steamed into us we sucked them in and battered fuck out of them. Still no police.

At the front of the Palace fans was a fat half-caste fella in a sheepskin. He stopped just short of a right-hander and obviously realised what they were piling into was not what they had thought they were going to be piling into. He sharply diverted sideways and escaped the bashing that his followers copped.

'He's Palace's main man,' said a bloke standing next to me.

Well, that about sums this lot up, I thought, as he waddled off to the far corner flag. Fighting was breaking out all over as the residents of Tooting and Mitcham bashed every Palace fan in sight. Palace were terrified, as their quiet afternoon turned into a bad dream. One of our lot was in the goalmouth spanking a Palace boy who, in his panic to get away, had got tangled up in the netting. He squirmed, flipped and gasped like a captured fish as his tormentor aimed kicks at his head, belly and bollocks.

Finally the police arrived and stemmed the anarchy, putting the customary ring of blue around the now outnumbered and shaken Palace contingent. Some of them knew some of us. They were baffled.

'What's going on? What's Man U and Chelsea doing together?' one asked.

'Tonking you wankers,' was the reply.

The police really did get a grip on the situation and there was no further serious fighting for the rest of the game, which Palace won. It was about the only thing that had gone to plan for them.

The Palace fans were allowed to leave the ground first and the police attempted to hold us in whilst they exited, but we were having none of it. We followed them out and in the street tailed them away from Sandy Lane.

'I bet they go back the way they came,' said Jimmy, a tall, ginger-haired Man United fan. He suggested we nip down the side streets and intercept them on Figgs Marsh. We did exactly that. Standing on the corner of the street which led directly on to the open green spaces which were Figgs Marsh, I looked around. There were about fifty of us making up a firm with about two hours' experience of fighting together, but it was like we'd been a unit for years. Jimmy had taken command and led from the front. There, about one hundred yards away, was the Palace firm. They appeared to be waiting for us. They were gluttons for punishment, but there was a good hundred of them and I suppose they fancied their chances.

'Nice and slowly!'

Jimmy stepped forward with an exaggerated slow and plodding walk. We all copied. We got to the main road that separated us and a load more stood up from a small wall they had been sitting on. They had not been visible earlier, so it was beginning to look like a two-hundred-strong gang we were crossing the road to meet. They made no move. No move to run and no move to charge us. It was obvious they were not used to this sort of thing. We were now amongst them and not a word had been spoken. It was almost embarrassing.

We didn't quite know what to do either. But then I heard the unmistakable sound of a whack of a fist on a face and a Palace fan was lying spark out on the pavement. Jimmy stood over him, poised to take out the next Palace fan to move in his direction. Then the rest of us just hit out at the nearest Palace face to us. It was a bit too cold and calculated for me. Football violence, thus far, had been all about the heat of the moment. The delay before tearing into them smacked of bullying. It was patently obvious that the Palace boys did not understand the rules. They had the sense to run and, tellingly, we made no attempt at a chase. But what happened next amazed me and really did seal their fate that day. Because we didn't chase, they stopped and took a look at us. I expect they thought, 'Hang on, there's not that many, and some of them are only kids – let's stand and fight.' But events took a nasty turn when the rest of our mob, which was about three times the size in numbers and included the Paddies and other loonies from the building site, appeared behind them, having waited at the train station for a while.

The Palace fans knew they were in shit street and panic set in on a large scale. They bolted. Not as a mob. Each individual decided at the same time that he would make his own bid to extricate himself from this dire situation. They should have stayed together and fought, or even stayed together and not fought. It was like the hunt had come to Figgs Marsh, with a couple of hundred foxes running here, there and everywhere, being pursued by packs of hounds savouring the kill. Twenty or so Palace fans dashed down a side street, failing to notice the No Through Road sign, and suffered an uncertain fate there. I saw only Mitcham boys walk back out. Others legged it across the grass area, hoping to make the relative safety of Tooting Junction station. It was a sight to behold, the Paddies, in their national dress of donkey jackets and Wellington boots, running awkwardly across the grass but one by one felling the terrified folk of Croydon. I half expected them to produce shovels from inside their donkey jackets and to start whacking the Palace fans on the deck. I'd like to be able to add that they were chanting 'Hello, hello, Wimpey aggro, Wimpey aggro, hello', but they were not.

One particular Palace fan ran across my path. I could easily have tripped him but didn't. Our eyes met and I recognised him from Mitcham. He knew who I was and I knew who he was. We almost smiled at one another. I had no wish to see him get kicked to fuck, and he got away safely.

After a while – it must have seemed like eternity for the Palace lot – the sound of sirens hailed the arrival of the police and we disappeared sharpish in the direction of a local housing estate and a pub we knew. Glancing back at Figgs Marsh, we saw it was like the scene of a battlefield: dozens of motionless bodies strewn across it, police running over to them, helping some to their feet, calling for ambulances for others. Back in the pub, we were laughing and joking about how the Palace had come unstuck against the most unlikely football mob of all when a couple of boys arrived and said that two Palace fans had been stabbed in the riot and were in a serious way. It took the edge off the day a bit. Palace hadn't deserved that, in my book. We were not up against Leeds or someone. They were our quarry for the day, but it was like angling. When we had caught them, we should have just thrown them back in. Lots of rumours went around as to who had carried out the knifings and over the next few days quite a few of the local lads were hauled in by the police. To my knowledge no one was charged and fortunately the injured boys recovered. Nevertheless, it was a nasty end to what had been a fun day out for almost all of those concerned.

Some seasons later we played the Palace at Selhurst Park. As I explained earlier, this fixture was really a day off for the boys, and I was happily standing in the Holmesdale End with a couple of mates when a small group of Palace fans squared up to us. At the front was my acquaintance from Mitcham whom I had not seen since the day on Figgs Marsh when he had run past me in an effort to escape the marauding Irishmen. Again he recognised me. Perhaps he had become a bit of a face down at Selhurst Park, because he immediately gave it the large one.

'Yer fucking mugs! You Chelsea are all mouth,' he snarled, doing the wankers sign under my nose.

His Palace cronies stood behind, laughing. I shoved him hard in the chest and he toppled backwards into his mates.

'Fuck off, you dozy little prick. If you want it, let's have it. But don't stand there mouthing off in front of yer mates.'

He appeared shocked by what I thought was a relatively mild reaction. Maybe he had taken my inaction that day on Figgs Marsh as a sign of weakness. Who knows? He definitely knew that he'd run into me around Mitcham sooner or later, so it was a strange call altogether.

'I know where you live. I'll be round to see ya,' was his parting shot as he edged away.

'Please do! Key's under the mat – let yourself in,' I shouted after him, and his mates were laughing again – only this time at him.

About a year after that incident, this same Palace fan killed a Swansea supporter in Wales. I think he knifed him. Perhaps he had been tooled up the day we had had words and that had given him the initial courage to front us up. Anyway, he got life and I never heard of him again until one day, not too long ago, I was told that he had hanged himself in prison. A very, very sad end to two young lives.

Bill Shankly is famous for having said that football is not a matter of life or death – it's much more important than that. Football violence certainly isn't. For someone to die because he supports a different team from someone else would be laughable if it weren't so sad. 'Pathetic hypocrite,' I hear you say, 'regretting the death of fans when you spent much of the last thirty years tearing up and down the country bashing people up or being bashed up.' The best analogy I can offer is boxing. Two opponents willingly and knowingly fight each other. They badly want to win and keep their reputations intact, but they definitely don't want to kill one another. Boxers do it for money. We do it for the buzz. And the buzz is addictive. But it is nothing personal. Most of the time.

NINE

My Mate Denton

Today is the start of a new season and Chelsea are at home to Everton. It's the morning of the game and I'm rushing around like a blue-arsed fly unpacking my suitcase. Mandy and I have just got back from a two-week break in Italy.

'Take my stuff up the dry-cleaners, will ya Mart?' asks Mandy.

'You're fucking joking, I hope! I'm trying to get meself straight so I can get down the Bridge.'

I haven't missed a start in over ten years and I'm not going to begin now. The first game always has a very special atmosphere. There is a high level of expectancy about how the team will perform, and you get the chance to weigh up any new signings. Each year Chelsea fans think this will be their season. Each year Chelsea fans are wrong. But most of all it's about getting in the boozer and catching up with your mates. It's funny, but most football fans have two sets of mates – their pals at home and their pals at football. Different sorts of mate, too. Some of the people you knock about with at football you would not choose to socialise with at home and vice versa. In some ways you don't know the guys at football that well. You've never met their mums, dads, girlfriends or wives; you've never been to their houses. You may not know what job they do (although in the '80s it was even money they were undercover Fulham CID), but because of the heightened experiences you have shared, a bond is formed. You take risks together and depend on each other for your physical well-being. Mates at home may only find themselves in these relationship-binding dangerous situations once or twice in a lifetime. For football mates it's every other week.

Today we're in the White Hart, down the corridor in the back bar. It is jammed solid and murder getting a drink, but you wouldn't have it any other way. Every one of us who walks in the door is grinning from ear to ear and gets a raucous welcome. It's only been a few weeks but we behave like we've all just got out of jail. 'Hear about Kev? Married. Says he's giving the football a rest', and 'Mark's been nicked – doing a stretch in Dover'. Soon you are up to date and you discuss the team, the ground and the chairman. Someone says they saw Greenaway up the road and he was wearing a syrup. Roars of laughter. We trot off to the ground. There's a good crowd and the Shed is in full voice. Everton win by one goal to nil. Same old story. We're going to struggle again. Frankly, the team looked awful. We trudge back to the White Hart, where we indulge in much moaning. A crowd of boys we know by sight bursts into the bar and they tell us excitedly that Chelsea are about to ambush Everton at Earls Court station. This cheers everyone up and we all leave half-empty glasses and scamper across to the tube station.

The ambushing of rival supporters was becoming quite common on the London Underground network and beyond. Natural, really. The Old Bill were progressively tightening up in the grounds but the further away from the arena you went, the less police presence you would find. More adventurous Chelsea firms started to leave the game early – or even not attend at all – and travel home on the route that the away supporters would use half an hour or so later. They think they are out of danger and that the day's fighting is over when the doors open at Earls Court or some such station and two hundred Chelsea pile in at them. They are shocked and trapped. The element of surprise is usually enough to finish them off. My pal Time Warp Terry told me about a time when three or four vanloads followed a coach of some northern team or other all the way to the first service station on the M1 in order to surprise the unsuspecting fans.

Today we spring off the tube at Earls Court. To me it is

obvious what's happening because I know all the faces. To an outsider it looks like a busy platform on a late Saturday afternoon. No colours, no singing, no groups. People standing singly or in twos, facing different directions. Two policemen are at the bottom of the stairs at the far end of the platform. The next train pulls in and it's full of Chelsea too. This is the worst-kept secret in south London. I'm thinking about fucking off.

'Why the big turnout for Everton?' I ask Peter Stevens, who is subtly motioning with his hands for the new arrivals to mingle in with the crowd and keep stumm.

'First game of the season, I suppose. Everyone's been a bit bored during the summer and having a go at the mickey mousers is as good a start as any,' is his informed analysis.

Everton are no pushovers; in fact, they are a lot more game than their neighbours Liverpool. The Anfield boys rarely turn up at Chelsea and are not known for their rucking abilities away from home. Goodison Park, on the other hand, can be a naughty place to visit and their firm are big and vicious. Over the last couple of seasons, stories have been filtering through about how their boys have been giving a good account of themselves all over the country, including London.

A train pulls in on the opposite platform. Jerry from Kilburn, who is for some reason known as Jerry Kilburn, stands at the door of one carriage as it opens.

'They're on here,' he whispers, flicking his head in the direction of the far end of the platform. 'Everton! They're in the top two carriages – with all of two Old Bill!'

Silently but purposefully the platform empties, and almost everyone boards the train. Still no one has noticed anything suspicious. Never one to rush when dawdling will do, I am left standing looking in at my mates after the doors have shut on me. The train isn't moving.

'What are you doing there, you scouse wanker?' asks Peter Stevens through the glass doors. Very funny, Pete. 'Lost yer bottle?' he continues. I smile back. Other Chelsea fans in the carriage pick up on this and, not knowing me from Adam, think Peter is genuinely digging out a scouser.

'Scouse wanker!' shouts one.

'Frightened to get on?' taunts his mate.

'These doors open and you're dead!' threatens another Chelsea fan, pushing himself to the front.

Peter and the boys are creasing up laughing and I simply smile back at my tormentors. This makes them almost frenzied. The doors open and I step on. The Chelsea half-wits step back. If this is how they deal with a solitary Everton fan, I'm not too happy about them tagging along with us. I lay on the cockney accent a bit thick.

'Well, boys, I didn't quite catch what you were saying. Could you repeat it, please?'

'Sorry, mate,' they replied in unison. 'We thought you was a scouser.'

The whole carriage has a good laugh at this interlude and the train pulls away. As we pass the steps I see four coppers; the Everton escort has departed! Chelsea are passing down through the middle of the train, moving from carriage to carriage, ever closer to the Everton firm. We are a few carriages behind but we can hear the off. Chelsea are in their compartment. Our stomachs are dancing. The train stops at Kensington High Street and we jump out and charge up the platform to the front. It is carnage already, with a few scousers stretched out on the floor and others cowering behind seats. Some are sobbing and pleading for mercy. Chelsea are taking turns to rush into the carriage, kick and punch everyone in sight and then jump back off to let others have a go. There is almost an orderly queue forming.

This goes on for a good five minutes and there is no attempt by Everton at retaliation. Mind you, they are well outnumbered and probably think their only hope is that we get tired or the police turn up. Why doesn't the driver or the guard close the doors and drive off? No way, that's them disappearing up the stairs. One Chelsea boy is swinging on the hanging supports with two hands and volleying Everton fans with his boots. They already look unconscious to me. I decide to piss off before someone gets hurt. We're at the top of the stairs and the police flash past, truncheons pulled. Someone is going to have a go at Chelsea after all.

The papers loved this one. 'CHELSEA THUGS IN AMBUSH' was the headline in my Sunday tabloid. It was a new season and the press were relieved that nothing had changed. The fighting had taken place on the public transport system, which conjured up images of frightened nuns and screaming babies being thrown on to the tracks. Good copy. We are sick animals and a scourge on society, they say. Fair enough. But who tells the press what they are? Who were the people who created league tables of football hooliganism? Who built up games to such an extent that if there hadn't been trouble it would have caused severe embarrassment for both sides? Who reported incidents that definitely did not occur? Who whips up English nationalism every few years? There are no excuses for what we do. But let's get things into perspective. During the week following the trouble, a press conference was held on a disused tube station. Displayed along the platform was a selection of weapons that had supposedly been seized or left at the scene of the incident. These weapons included machetes, samurai swords and baseball bats. Really, officer? Do they seriously think the public swallows this garbage? Try taking a tube ride with a crossbow or a samurai sword and see how far you get.

The following week we were away at Spurs. The usual massive firm turned out for this one and we met at Liverpool Street station and caught a rattler to Bruce Grove. Three hundred or so alighted but organisation was poor. The first hundred or so leapt on to the platform and went straight out into the road instead of waiting for us all to get together. They galloped off down Tottenham High Road, chasing a small group of Yids. Soon they were running back with a serious Spurs mob in pursuit. Give Spurs their due: they came straight into us, but the Chelsea faces at the back could not get at them because our own over-enthusiastic boys were forming a cushion between us and them. Horses and dogs arrived, accompanied by funny men in black who pushed Tottenham on to one pavement and us on to another. The police walked down the middle of the road, holding up all the traffic until we were safely deposited in the Park Lane end which had been set aside for visiting fans. Occasionally the dog-handlers slackened the dogs' leads so the Alsatians could have a nip at some football fan's arse. It delighted the police when the dogs ripped out the seat of some poor bloke's Levis. Perhaps the sight of young male buttocks gave them a thrill.

In the ground, I could see the turnout was even better than I had thought. A few years before, we had come seriously unstuck here at White Hart Lane. A lot of our boys had been locked out of the ground and the ones inside had endured a real spanking. We were determined that this should not happen again.

We made our way down to the front, by the corner flag, where Babs and company were exchanging banter with the Tottenham main crew on the other side of the fence.

'You lot run a bit early, didn't ya?'

'We didn't run anywhere,' replied Babs calmly. 'You chased a few of our muppets up the road. The rest of us hadn't even got out the station.'

I recognised the Yid engaging Babs. He had turned up once with a bunch of fifty or so mates at Scamps night-club in Sutton. They had let everyone know they were Tottenham and they were looking for some well-known Cockney Reds who came from the area. There had been a stand-off but nothing had really happened. Playground stuff. He was a name up at Spurs, organising their away travel. I suspected he was all mouth and fancied that if there had been no fence between us he'd have been a lot more subdued. Unable to rile Babsy, he turned to us and started winding us up.

'Pooper going, mate?'

He was implying that we were frightened. But he was wasting his time with us. Chelsea fans were the masters of piss-taking and had an answer for everything.

One Saturday at Chelsea, we were in the North Stand taunting a Southampton firm who, safe in the knowledge that half of the Fulham police force were protecting them, made out they wanted to get at us. The police held them back. Most of the Chelsea were incensed and were shouting and screaming at them.

'Don't bother with all that,' said Chris, a tall, blond lad from Epsom. 'This really winds them all up.'

He leant towards the Southampton boys, smiling, held one arm aloft, crooked his little finger and wiggled it at them. Chelsea went deadly quiet and all turned to the Southampton and did the same. Southampton went quiet too; they didn't know what it meant. Neither did Chris – but it did the trick. Assuming this was some secret insult of the most dire type, they went apeshit.

Another time at Portsmouth, Chelsea were ripping the seats out and launching them at a line of police who were trying to quell a potential pitch invasion. Every now and then a police-man went down as a flying seat caught him in the face, but one copper in particular, a huge, red-haired man mountain, stood there defiantly, his hands locked behind his back. Chris again got a chant going – 'Knock down Ginger, knock down Ginger' – and urged the crowd to aim the seats solely at the fat copper. He ducked, the crowd roared 'Knock down Ginger, knock down Ginger' again, and then his hands were around his head, protecting himself from this hail of missiles. Finally he ran for cover and the crowd chanted, 'Shit out Ginger, shit out Ginger.'

The Tottenham game ended in a 2–2 draw and we hung about outside, gathering as many of us together as we could for the long hike back up the road to the Seven Sisters Under-ground station. As we turned the corner on to Tottenham High Road, it kicked off. Spurs came roaring into us. No hesitation. Boots, fists and nuts going nineteen to the dozen. People were punching anyone who came within striking distance and no one really knew who was who. Lads who dropped to the floor were being kicked around like footballs. They were down and it was unlucky. It was one of those fights where there was no time or space to think – just to lash out. The police were soon back to put the human barrier between us and we continued up the road, each mob eyeballing the other. Another fight erupted behind us, where a Spurs gang had crept up and picked off the Chelsea stragglers. We turned to face them and a stocky bloke who was at the front of their lot strode straight into us. Before we knew it he had put two of us down. Fists then rained down on him and he sank to his knees. His mates froze. If they'd all been like him, they would have gone straight through us.

'Come on, boys, you can do better than that,' smiled Babsy.

The police pushed us forwards to rejoin the main Chelsea contingent. Outside Tottenham nick, the Old Bill led us away from Seven Sisters tube, choosing instead to lead us up to Tottenham Hale. They blocked the road behind us and held the Spurs fans back. This seemed to satisfy them and the police escort disappeared. By the time we reached the entrance to the station, though, a Spurs crew had materialised behind us. There were a hundred or so Yids, led by the gobby Cockney Red hater from the ground and Sammy Skyves. Skyves had been a face at Tottenham for a long time and, along with Eccles at Chelsea, Gardner at West Ham and Johnny Hoy at Arsenal, was among the first crop of football ruckers to achieve London-wide fame.

This time we didn't hesitate and tore into them. The sheer weight of numbers forced Tottenham to beat a hasty retreat. The boys in blue were back as quickly and as quietly as they had disappeared, and we were bundled into the station. I suspected we'd just been set up and that the police were giving Tottenham a free hand, but you can never tell. The police constantly reacted to these situations in mysterious ways. Most of the time I suspected it was incompetence, but there were a number of instances I knew of, especially out of town, where they had led the away fans into ambushes.

Sometimes, however, they were happy to see us give their local boys a leathering. In the early '80s, the Chelsea coaches would pull into various towns, away from where the football had been played, for a Saturday night's drinking. On one of these occasions, three coaches from Battersea, full of Chelsea's main boys, arrived in a cathedral city. The police greeted them in the coach park on their arrival. They were friendly and joking.

'By all means have a drink here, lads. But we don't want any trouble. We'll be down on you like a ton of bricks.'

'No sweat, officer,' agreed a well-known organiser of the time.

'By the way,' the policeman continued in his country burr,

'the lads here think they are a bit special. Know what I mean? Teach them a bit of a lesson if you like. Shake them up a bit. Mind you, no damage to property and no hurting anyone seriously. Understand?'

The Chelsea boys nodded vigorously. It's not often you get the police's blessing for a tear-up, unless it's a set-up. The policemen then gave them directions to the pub where the local herberts drank. This is all true. Chelsea ambled up to the pub, flushed the locals out and chased them all over town for a good half-hour before carrying on drinking for the night in their boozer.

We squeeze like sardines into a waiting train at Tottenham Hale station and rattle off. First stop Seven Sisters. Doors open. Wall-to-wall Tottenham. A moment in time is frozen as we look at one another. Two game mobs, inches apart. Someone shouts, 'Yes!' Sounds like Eccles's throaty roar. We take the initiative and charge them, forcing them back up the platform, and then chase them up the down escalators. This is tiring and some fans are running up the non-moving middle of the escalator. Soon the battle is being fought out in the street. Everyone is picking up bricks, lumps of wood, newspaper headline boards, whatever they can lay their hands on. A solitary policeman is helpless among the fracas. He arrests an innocent, inoffensive fan and busies himself with him rather than taking any mortal risks. This really is a full-scale riot for the papers. It's been going on for five minutes, and that's a long time for a fight on this scale. Most football violence is over before it has begun, but not this one. Me and the lads from Mitcham decide to exit. The Old Bill must get here soon and they will be nicking people at random. We've had a ruck, Chelsea are on top, and so we split.

Later on that same season we had Arsenal at home, and as usual we all met up in the White Hart. Word had gone around that Arsenal were going to turn up in force this year. Sometimes they did, sometimes they didn't. We waited in the pub until 2.30 p.m., but no show. We walked up to the North Stand to test the police's foolproof system for preventing home fans from gaining entry to the away end.

'Who d'you support?' growled one burly policeman.

'Arsenal,' we lied.

He pushed us through on to a colleague who touched various parts of our bodies in what was meant to be a search for weapons and we were in.

Inside it was obvious that many, many more Chelsea boys had penetrated this sophisticated screening process. Steve Rutland, a Chelsea fan from east London, came down to the bottom of the North Stand to meet us.

'There's about thirty Arsenal at the top of the stairs. But it looks like their young lot,' he informed us.

'Any Chelsea with 'em?' I asked.

Steve said there wasn't, so we decided to wander up and have a look. Twenty of us walked up the slope which ran down the back of the north terrace. The Arsenal lot were sitting on the concrete steps at the top, looking down.

'Hello boys,' said Rutland as we stood in front of them.

With that some of them got to their feet and dissolved into the crowd.

'You won't be so brave when our main lot turns up,' said one of the Gooners.

'We thought you were the main boys,' I returned.

A couple of police, sensing a row in the making, gently ushered us away and stood between us.

Bodies were flooding into the ground now and I could see more and more Chelsea mobbing up where we stood. I needed a lag so made my way to the toilets. 'A fucking disgrace' is the only way to describe these things. There are never enough in any ground. They are made of cheap breeze block with a tin roof that leaks water on your head whether it's raining or not. A metal trough runs the length of the shack with a couple of holes that collect the second-hand beer and dog-ends. Scores of people crush into these temples of piss, and those who can't fit in slash up the walls outside. You are guaranteed to come out with waterlogged shoes due to someone pissing on you or because the trough has overflowed. Football fans only piss. Did you know that? We don't possess bowels and we don't shit. There are no cubicles whatsoever. If you were caught short, it was tough. Remember, these facilities were meant to cater for 'real' football fans – not just us animals. Disgusting. How we never contracted yellow fever or green monkey disease, I will never know.

Walking back on to the terrace, I stood in a gap which I soon realised had appeared between the Arsenal and Chelsea fans.

'Come on, ya Chelsea wanker!'

I turned around. Standing behind me was a young black man aged about eighteen.

'Come on, ya Chelsea wanker – let's do it!' he repeated.

I stared back at him.

'You talking to me?'

'Go on, Denton, do him!' bayed the gang with the black boy.

I had unwittingly walked straight into the middle of a stand-off between the Gooners' main firm and a Chelsea firm.

'Have you ever thought about joining the National Front?' I enquired of the black man standing three feet away.

'I can't, I'm black,' the boy answered in a matter-of-fact way.

It was as if I had asked him to lend me some money and he was sorry but he was unable to do so because he was skint. Both sides burst out laughing at our strange little exchange. The police moved the Arsenal boys down a few steps and stood between us, and we continued to trade insults and take the piss out of one another. The police didn't mind the language in those days. As long as there were no punches being thrown, they were happy to ignore it and watch the game.

Steve Rutland tapped me on the shoulder.

'See the spade you had words with? He's called Denton and he's one of the top Gooners these days.'

'So fucking what?'

I couldn't give a shit who he was. To me he was a teenage sooty with a lot of front.

At the end of the game we stood at the top of the terrace and waited for Arsenal to leave. They were grouping together to maximise the numbers and the police led them out of the terrace. We were standing around the steps that led down from the West Stand and, as usual, the police led the away fans out of the ground but provided no cover at the sides. We steamed into them and every single Gooner took off. We chased them out on to the street, where a big Chelsea firm was waiting. Arsenal backed up on to the footpath outside the North Stand entrance. A big Greek-looking fella came running over from across the road and thumped the geezer standing alongside me, laying him out. Three or four Chelsea boys jumped on him but he managed to shake them off and ran down the road, followed by what was left of the Gooners' mob.

Walking now towards Fulham Broadway station, I couldn't believe my luck when I saw Denton bouncing down the middle of the road, seemingly without a care in the world. I quickly pulled up alongside him and BANG. I cracked him a beauty on the side of his head. He didn't hang around, diving in and out of the crowd and disappearing into the night. 'Shit,' I thought, 'I've lost him.'

Looking over at the huge queue by the station, I decided to walk down to Parsons Green station and pick up a train there. As I walked down the side of the green that leads to the station, who did I see in front of me? Yes. Denton again.

'Oi, wanker!' I shouted at the top of my voice. He looked around, clocked me and shot off like he had a rocket up his arse. I bumped into Steve Rutland by the station and he said that Denton had motored past him at a hundred miles an hour.

A couple of years later we were playing up at Newcastle and Arsenal were travelling to Leeds. Hanging around King's Cross, waiting for our train, we were approached by some Chelsea juniors who ran up and told us that a small firm of Gooners were lounging around outside the station. A few of us strolled out to the taxi rank to take a look. There he was again. My mate Denton. Now *the* face at the Arsenal. He looked over at me, turned and tore up the road, his mates in tow.

We had a boring day up at St James' Park but did meet up with Rutland, who told us that Denton had returned from his early-morning run to the station concourse only to bump into Melvyn. One of Icky's followers, Melvyn had made his name with his virtuoso performance at Cardiff some years before. He walked over to Denton and put a gun to his head. All those who saw it said his eyes popped out of his head and he seemed to go weak at the knees. Denton was not to know that Melvyn's tool was only a starting pistol. Later, on the last leg home, we met some Gooners on the tube. It was late, we were fucked, they were fucked and instead of squaring up we had a chat. They described how Leeds had chased the Arsenal mob all over town. All in all, a bad day for my mate Denton.

TEN

Dawn Raids

The early 1980s were arguably the years when soccer-related violence, or fear of it, reached its peak. The boys were now dressing like tennis stars, sporting designer labels such as Ellesse, Tacchini, Fila and Lacoste. Terrace disturbances resembled clashes between armies of John McEnroe clones and hordes of Bjorn Borg lookalikes. Hooliganism was trendy. Not just with the hooligans themselves, but with the outside world. Books written by academics were beginning to appear, in which they attempted to find sociological explanations for the behaviour. Desmond Morris, whom we all knew as the boring bald-headed bloke who presented TV's *Zoo Time* when we were kids, wrote a book in which he tried to relate it all back to animal instincts.

The television industry even got in on the act. Firstly they made a documentary about Millwall's firm in which a chap who went by the name of Harry the Dog was introduced to the world. Millwall fans were shown wearing surgical masks and the programme focused on a particular crew that called themselves 'Treatment'. The people featured in this programme seemed positively harmless compared to the real thing I had encountered some years earlier. I heard a story about Harry the Dog which may or may not be true but is worth recounting anyway. A young Australian student came to London to study at one of our colleges and found digs in sunny Deptford. On his first Saturday in south-east London he decided to pop into a nearby pub for a pint and a spot of lunch. He did not know that Millwall were playing at home that day and that this boozer was full of their boys. If he had known, it would not have meant anything to him anyway. The pub was packed, and he had to elbow his way through to the bar. In the squeeze, he accidentally knocked a man's drink over.

'I'm terribly sorry, mate. Let me get you another,' apologised the student.

'Do you know who I am?' asked the man menacingly.

The student shook his head.

'I'm Harry the Dog.'

The pub fell silent. All eyes were on Millwall's famed warrior and the student.

'And I'm Larry the Lamb, pleased to meet you,' smiled the Australian, extending his hand.

More silence. Then canine Harry smiled, the pub broke up in laughter and he bought the student a drink. Nice tale, anyway.

The other television documentary was a little time later and centred on the various firms at West Ham. This production came over as much less contrived than the Millwall study and did a lot to raise the media profile of football gangs.

More than anything else, though, the 1980s were when football hooliganism went international. Although there had been some notable riots at England matches abroad in the '70s, it was during the '80s that the country convinced itself it was wrestling with demons on a par with the Northern Ireland troubles. Each successive World Cup became the top item on *News at Ten*, not because of any fantastic performances from our national side but because they were reporting on the latest activities of our fans. Much of it was non-news. England camps for fans set up. Fans put in tents. Fans drunk but good-humoured. After the game, bar gets smashed up. Italian fans taunt English fans. Running fights. Fairly anti-social. Not good for the country's image on the international stage. But front-page news? Every day for weeks?

I don't think so. Methinks there was a bit more to it. At the risk of sounding like the aforementioned Mr Morris, I think the whole idea of thousands of young Englishmen marching around Europe stirs something in the national psyche. That Commonwealth, imperialist, Falklands thing. Most won't admit it and will outwardly condemn it, but the sight of the English marauding through Europe causes them to smile inwardly. They might not like it but they can't help it. I call it the Alf Garnett syndrome. He was a tremendously popular figure in the 1960s and '70s and the literary classes and media types said it was because he was a parody of a working-class bigot. He made the working classes wake up to their own archaic prejudices. We were laughing *at* him, they told us. Bollocks. We were laughing *with* him, and so were they. He articulated beautifully what most people, from all classes, thought but wouldn't say. I see it now, executives in their company Saabs, driving around London, probably subscribing to an equal opportunities personnel policy at their place of work – but all black people do for them, in truth, is remind them to switch on their central locking as they ease along Clapham High Road.

I never got into following England abroad at all. From what I gather, Chelsea dominated it and Icky, in particular, was a focal point. But every time an outbreak of trouble occurs I am taken aback by the level of outcry and righteous indignation. Theories to explain the behaviour abound. Personally I don't think there is a lot more to it than the fact it's an excuse for a good ruck in new surroundings and the opportunity to perform in front of a global audience. From the South London Press to CNN in one fell swoop.

Having said that, there is probably a little bit of truth in the national identity theory which is frequently offered up. My generation was particularly infused with the whole Great Britain concept. Our dads fought in the war and spoke often and proudly about it; our weekend TV viewing was dominated by films about the war and Jack Hawkins breaking out of POW camps; and our playground games consisted of joining arms and chanting 'Who wants to play war?'. In the classroom we were taught about the achievements of Nelson, Wellington, Churchill and the royal family – and the debt of gratitude we owed them. We were taught to be proud of the Empire and how we had educated those inferior races around the world and taught them how to better themselves. That's how it was. And then, all of a sudden, that all changed. The Union Jack was a racist emblem, the British exploited and plundered all over, war was bad and blacks were equal. I'm not saying that the first set of premises is right. I'm saying you can't have it both ways. If you switch a whole set of values in the middle of a generation, it's inevitable there will be a kickback. I think the international football hooliganism thing was one manifest-ation of that kickback.

No one made a TV film about Chelsea but a lot of unwel-come TV and newspaper coverage was shortly to come our way. No one could argue with the fact that the West Ham chaps made famous in that TV production were the most prominent firm of the 1980s. They called themselves the InterCity Firm (ICF for short) and really had the media creaming their pants when they started to leave ICF calling cards at the scenes of their rucks. Their members ranged from boys in their early teens to grandfathers approaching fifty, and when they played Chelsea or any other London club they would turn out in force. Around this time there was not a mob to match them, although, unlike Chelsea, they didn't fare as well in the further-flung parts of the country. But West Ham never let you down. They'd walk our streets, drink in our pubs and even sit in our seats in the ground. They really were game.

One season they had thousands on all sides of the ground. We stood in the Shed open-mouthed. We couldn't believe the front of it. Outside they were organised with military preci-sion. They always managed to mob up outside grounds and avoid the perils of getting split up. The Old Bill treated them with respect tinged with a certain wariness and often left them to their own devices. Another time they came in the Shed end turnstiles but there was a scuffle in the forecourt area. The police pushed us back into the Shed and escorted the West Ham interlopers back out through the gates and on to the Fulham Road. The ICF simply split into smaller groups and came straight back in, paying at the turnstiles again. The police thought they had it sussed but West Ham were mobbing up again, stronger than before. We stood at the top of the steps on the edge of the Shed, aghast at the stupidity of the police, who were labouring under the impression that those naughty East-Enders were on a District Line train homeward bound – instead of gathering in great numbers around the turnstile area. There were a good hundred of them and the same number of us looking down from the top of the stairs. The Shed boys were in full song, swaying in the afternoon sun, oblivious to the fact that a vicious and dangerous West Ham firm were a few feet away and planning to run them all over the show.

The East End boys liked taking the Shed – it was good PR and it kept up morale. At the front of their mob was Gardner, easily recognisable by his trademark ginger hair. He had been around for years and was the acknowledged leader of the ICF, although in my very early football-going days I remember a chap by the name of Williams being the main face down at West Ham. They walked calmly to the top of the stairs. Gardner stopped a few steps below us and looked leisurely along the line of us, like a sergeant-major inspecting his troops.

'Good afternoon, gentlemen. The name is Gardner,' he grinned.

His announcement had the desired effect on some. I felt a draught behind me as a few bodies sneaked off into the relative safety of the Shed. If a professional observer had been present, he would have thought what a nice-mannered chap Gardner was and how civilised the proceedings were between the two gangs. The intention, however, was for the utterance of the very name Gardner to be enough to scatter the Chelsea masses.

To me, though, the name Gardner didn't have quite the same ring as Kray or Capone, and obviously someone very near me thought the same way. Crack. He took the punch full in the face but didn't go down. His boys were not so brave and skidded down the steps, over the turnstiles and back on to the forecourt. Gardner, for the moment a leader with no followers, reluctantly followed. The Adelaide, Imperial, Nell Gwynn, Rising Sun and Wheatsheaf pubs had just spilled their human contents out on to the street. West Ham literally bumped straight into a fairly large but loose and boozed-up Chelsea mob. Most of them ran or melted, mistakenly thinking that West Ham were charging out to give it to them. Little did they know that Gardner had just been chinned and that this lot were in retreat. West Ham were heartened by this Chelsea reaction, the one they had been expecting, and proceeded to splatter the fifty or so hardcore Chelsea who stood and had it with them.

In our defence, we were well depleted that day. The police had raided the houses of a dozen or so of Chelsea's known faces and arrested them. The television news had been full of pictures of burly policemen kicking in doors of houses in the early hours of the morning and leading out sleepy but shocked alleged hooligans to waiting vans. Following them up the garden paths was a stream of policemen carrying an array of weapons which the public (and potential future jurors) were meant to believe were employed in their terrace antics. Crossbows, machetes, blow torches. Yeah, sure. You half expected them to bring out an Exocet missile code-named Zigger Zagger. I wondered if this was the very same arsenal as the one they had wheeled out after the Everton ambush.

When the reporter said a man had been taken from Tunbridge Wells, we all knew immediately it was Icky. He was a likeable geezer who, ever since that day a decade before when he had piped up at Sunderland, had become a bit of a legend at Chelsea. He had sort of broken away from the main Chelsea mob and done his own thing, which revolved around the coaches he ran from around the Kent area. Tales of these coach trips went down in folklore as the Icky convoy travelled around the land, causing havoc and having fun. There was a bit of snobbery towards him from some quarters at first. The older and more local Chelsea mobs refused to take someone from the sticks too seriously and I think they resented his rapid rise to prominence as his escapades became wilder and wilder. For my part, I liked him. He was good company, extremely funny and bitingly articulate. A real showman. He was Chelsea through and through and I'd rather be shoulder to shoulder with him in a punch-up than with some other Chelsea faces who have, before and since, set themselves up as top boys.

Icky stories are legion. He told me once about the time he ran two coaches up north and on the way home they decided to stop at a motorway service station. A couple of lads walked across the encased bridge that linked one area of the services with another on the other side of the motorway and spotted a couple of Leeds coaches unloading. They scooted back to the main lot and imparted the good news. Quietly they all walked across the bridge to meet up with their old enemy, but before they arrived on the other side, three unsuspecting men came trotting up the stairs. Icky quickly recognised one as Swallow, along with Gardner and Caz one of West Ham's best-known faces.

'Hello, lads,' Swallow muttered nervously, trying to work out who these eighty geezers were.

Chelsea could not believe their luck. In front of them was the cream of the West Ham mob and for once the numbers were in Chelsea's favour. Swallow's mind was working over-time. Did he run and leave his two pals? Should all three of them run and hope for the best? Or perhaps this mob were northerners and he could take a chance and front it out?

'Hello, Swallow,' said one of the Chelsea.

'Fuck me,' he was thinking. 'They know who I am.' Then he clocked a Chelsea face in the crowd. 'Shit, you're Chelsea,' he thought aloud, spinning around, and you couldn't see the three of them for dust. Some of the Chelsea lot gave chase but the majority were doubled up with laughter. Swallow and his chums shot out into the car park and carried on running down the hard shoulder of the motorway until they disappeared from view. A few days later Icky rang Swallow and pretended to be the Old Bill, warning him he was going to be issued with a speeding ticket for exceeding 70mph on the motorway whilst travelling in the wrong direction!

Tony Jones told me another cracking Icky tale. The Blues were up at Sunderland for a cup game and about ten of them had managed to lose the main body of Chelsea and the accompanying police escort after the game. They nipped away from the ground and went hunting for Sunderland fans. The group was well away from Roker Park when a police car screeched up beside them.

'Where do you lot think you're going?' demanded a uniform as he jumped out of the car.

'Good afternoon, officer. I do believe we are lost,' said Icky. 'We're trying to find our coach.'

'Well, they're bloody miles from here.'

At that the policeman radioed for a meatwagon and waited with this little crew until it arrived. When it did, he instructed the driver to take the Chelsea fans to the area where the away coaches had been parked up. In the van, Icky struck up a conversation with the driver.

'To be honest, I'm only a special,' the driver confided to him. 'I don't really know the area that well. Where is this coach park?'

'Don't worry, I'll show you.'

Icky turned and grinned widely to his mates. Eventually he saw a small Sunderland firm congregating on a street corner.

'This'll do. Stop here. I recognise it; we're just down the road there. Drop us here, please, mate.'

The police van stopped level with the Sunderland fans. The back doors burst open and Icky and company piled out and straight into the bemused Sunderland fans. Tyne and Wear police and Icky's mob in league together?

Hickmott's arrest, along with a bunch of other Chelsea boys, really did send shockwaves across not only Chelsea but all football mobs. Up and down the country firms worried about that early-morning shoulder on the door. Some other mobs did get arrested and half-hearted trials followed, but the police, it seemed, concentrated their efforts on the infamous Chelsea Headhunters. This was the showcase trial.

Headhunters. That's got a nice ring to it. Where this name came from I'll never know. Either the police (to sensationalise evidence) or the media (to liven up copy), I guess. We certainly never referred to ourselves as headhunters. We couldn't have imagined anything more naff. But this was a time when all the firms had names and we didn't. West Ham were the InterCity Firm, as mentioned earlier, because they travelled to away games on British Rail InterCity trains. I don't know if they have changed their name since privatisation. Leeds were the

Service Crew and Portsmouth were the 6.57 mob, after the time of their early-morning train. (All these links to the railways lead me to suspect that all these mobs consisted of closet trainspotters.) Before you knew it, everyone was called something. Small-time print shops were coining it, making up calling cards with names like Border City Firm, Zulu Warriors, Naughty Forty, BBC (Blades Business Crew or Beer Belly Crew, depending on the club), Guvnors, Aberdeen Casuals and many others.

The best handle of the lot, though, was Leicester, who christened themselves the Baby Squad. Big Baby Squad, I call them. Their mob is like a Bulgarian red wine or pie and mash – they don't travel too well. Apparently they got their name following a match at Leeds when their main boys (as usual) stayed at home. Outside the ground, Leicester's youngsters were left to defend themselves against the nationally feared Leeds firm and ended up running the home fans ragged. The youngsters were duly elevated to become the main Leicester firm, hence the Baby Squad. I've never rated Leicester as a mob, though. Unlike Forest, West Brom, Wolves and Birmingham, the other Midlands sides, Leicester have never turned up at the Bridge. Not once. They have plenty of bunny up there, though, and seem to enjoy the protection of their local police force. On more than one occasion the police have stood back and allowed them to steam into us and not lifted a finger. When we retaliate – wham, we're nicked. That sort of thing really gets me out of my pram.

Steve Hickmott and his so-called Headhunters had a high-profile trial at the Old Bailey, with Icky himself drawing a ten-year sentence at the end of it. It was a fit-up and a half in my book. The prosecution painted a picture of a malevolent neo-Nazi network of would-be murderers wreaking violence on innocent victims. They had private bank accounts where they stored cash to fund their activities and they networked with other overseas right-wing terror groups. All bollocks. Who'd let Hickmott look after their cash? Most of the time it was murder getting anyone at Chelsea to buy you a drink! Nazis? All the mobs went through a right-wing stage in the late '70s and early

'80s, but Chelsea were no worse than anyone else. It was said in court that Icky and his gang hated blacks. Tell that to Black Willie. Obviously the undercover police, whose evidence underpinned this whole trial, failed to notice this 6ft 6in black man weighing sixteen stone who travelled around with them. There were many others too. The National Front sold their paper outside the ground, but so did the Socialist Workers' Party. Racism was evident at Chelsea for a while but it was not the cement that bound us together in the way the media presented. The whole right-wing thing was a fad that passed.

The police wanted a fall guy. They knew that Icky, Ginger Terry and the others were not evil or a threat to society, but they needed to show Maggie they were on top of this malaise that had gripped the country's media so. Where better to start than Chelsea? Who better to start with than Icky? He was a thorn in the Old Bill's side. Not only was he organising Chelsea's away excursions every other week but he was the best-known face at England matches. Supporters from every club in England, Scotland and Wales knew him or had heard of him. So they stalked him with undercover detectives. Or should I say defectives. They did their research so badly they even had Ginger Terry down as the 'General', with Hickmott as his sidekick. Poor old Terry – he must be the first man in legal history sentenced to ten years' imprisonment for possessing a diary.

Two and a half years after their sentencing, all the boys were released and their convictions quashed after it was proved that the police had tampered with notebook evidence. The Chelsea boys were awarded damages but I do not recall any action being taken against the officers involved in this rather unsatisfactory initiative which the police themselves fittingly called 'Operation Own Goal'.

Some time before, Kevin, a known face at Chelsea, received a life sentence for allegedly being involved in a pub brawl in which a man was badly glassed. This was not even a football-related incident but the police and the media turned it into one and Kevin copped this disproportionate punishment. His sentence was reduced on appeal but he still did a ridiculous amount of bird for the crime he was supposed to have committed. It says a lot for our society when we bang up the likes of Icky, Ginger Terry and Kevin for a combined thirty years, when a wife murderer (who was apparently tormented by his deceased spouse but she's not here to tell her side of the story) or child molester rarely draws more than six or seven years.

With Hickmott inside and Babs and Eccles long gone, the Chelsea mob went into a rapid decline. The impact on morale, confidence and numbers was tangible. I recall going to Highbury on a Wednesday night and the best firm we could muster was about twenty geezers. When we left the ground we managed to dodge Arsenal's lot, embarrassed more than scared, but could hear them slapping the Chelsea hats and scarves all the way down to the tube. Sad and demeaning.

Icky's internment had created a vacuum and it was only a matter of time before someone came along and took on the job of holding Chelsea's mob together. Soon two people were putting themselves up for it: Tommy White, a small, wiry, bald-headed fella, and Sweeney. Sweeney assumed Icky's role of running the coaches. He loved a pound note, did Sweeney. Collecting them, that is, not spending them. He was known as a right tight-arse. Tommy White could always be found with a huge bloke by his side whom everyone knew as the Ox. His real name was Dave, and he came from Battersea. So, Tommy did the organising for the meets – what pub, what train or coach and what time – and Sweeney arranged the actual travel. Also coming to the fore at this time was Mark Cator. He came from Wandsworth originally but had married and moved to Dagenham, Essex, deep in Hammers country. If there is one team that Cator detests it's West Ham, so you can imagine how he felt about having to live among that lot. So these were the key figures at the front of the Chelsea lot, or at least the lot I was knocking around with.

Today we are hosts to Newcastle and a big row is on the cards. The Geordies were severely turned over a couple of seasons before, when the Chelsea boys bushwhacked two of their coaches at the Wandsworth Bridge roundabout, and they have never forgiven us for it. Word had gone around during the game that the ambush was planned for half an hour after the match at the bottom of Wandsworth Bridge. I must admit I thought this was another great idea from you know who, but I had to drive out that way on the route home, so me and my four mates kept an eye out for any activity. I'd parked as usual in a side street near to where the away coaches parked up, and as we approached the car we could hear the Geordies singing and shouting as the police escorted them to their transport. We tail-ended all the way up Townmead Road, as was always the case. The radio went on to break up the boredom of sitting in traffic and we listened transfixed to the match report. Strange, that. We had just sat through ninety minutes of shit but still had to listen to some broadcaster telling us how shit we were. We turned left on to the bridge over the Thames.

'Told ya,' said someone in the back, noticing a distinct lack of people anywhere. I could see in my mirror that two Newcastle coaches were about twenty vehicles behind and they hadn't been touched yet. The traffic started to move a bit and as I swung around the roundabout my headlights picked out silhouettes. Hundreds of them. Every fucking where. The centre of the roundabout, which was not visible from the bridge, was teeming with Chelsea. The inside of the roundabout was like an Indian reservation.

'Here we jolly well go,' I smiled, and I steered round the island for a second time. All hell broke loose. Bricks, bottles and lumps of concrete were pounded against the windows and the sides of the coaches. The second coach had braked suddenly and was embedded in a lamp-post on the pathway. The first coach was adrift in the middle of the road, having been stopped by what must have been between two and three hundred people blocking its path. The driver of the second coach opened the doors to let the Geordies get off and run for it but Chelsea clambered in and forced them to the back of the coach. The pressure of bodies seemed to make the back windscreen literally explode. The coach was shitting Geordies. Perhaps this is what is meant by Newcastle Brown. It was mayhem. Not wishing to get my collar felt, and with a protective eye on my prized Ford Capri, I whizzed off. I heard later that it was a good ten minutes before the police got the situation under control. The Newcastle fans had to make the long journey home bruised, battered and windowless. But they would not have been cold, because Geordies are big and tough and think nothing of wearing T-shirts in winter.

Today the Geordies have arrived nice and early and have plotted themselves in two pubs halfway down the King's Road. Funny how these northern sides – and even some London teams – think they are taking liberties by drinking in 'our' pubs. Get real. Yuppies, Sloane Rangers and people you recognise vaguely from 1970s sitcoms are the people who eat and drink on the King's Road, not Chelsea's boys. Mind you, I have a vague memory of standing in the Chelsea Potter as a teenager when Eccles and Greenaway were rowing over who was the better King Lear, Gielgud or Olivier.

Anyway, they are in these two pubs close together. We start to gather in a little boozer in a neighbouring backstreet. 'The Geordies are on the move!' shouts a spotter, throwing open the pub door. We all knock back our drinks and head off to the King's Road. I am in front and get my shoulder up against the door of the first pub for a dramatic and hopefully effective entrance. But the police do their usual appearing act and run into us with truncheons pulled. They are too busy pushing us down the road to notice that the hundred or so Chelsea at the back have attacked the pub opposite. The Geordies in here have shat themselves, jumping over the bar and under tables, although a few defend the bar with bottles. The police are now riding horses practically into the pubs and we split up to calm the situation down.

I meet up with Cator, Sweeney, Jeff Paine and Tommy White in a small boozer down the road. It seems that Tommy ran into the second pub on his own, a good ten seconds ahead of the rest, and motored straight into the Geordies. For his pains he had a bottle smashed over his head but he seems relatively unscathed. The story soon spreads and probably gets exaggerated along the way, but this enhances Tommy's reputation and cements his position as numero uno at Chelsea for the time being. The Newcastle mob receive a massive police escort to the ground and little is seen or heard of them for the rest of the day. One thing is for sure: the police won't be letting them go home over Wandsworth Bridge alone today.

Just the other side of Wandsworth Bridge stood the York Tavern, which for a while in the late '70s and early '80s became the main watering hole for Chelsea's most fanatic followers. We used it occasionally on the way home. It was far enough away from the ground not to figure in the police's security arrangements but the chances of away fans stumbling into this almost backstreet pub were slim (Geordies in coaches excluded). Purely by accident, though, I witnessed another huge set-to outside these premises and again I was sitting in a car. It was Friday evening and the height of the rush hour. I was with a black mate of mine, let's call him Leroy, because that was his name, and we had just finished work on doing up some flats in Battersea. We were stuck in the traffic opposite the old candle factory, edging down towards the famous Wandsworth roundabout. I could see that the York was looking lively, with scores of young men in England shirts drinking outside. I remembered that a lot of Chelsea boys were travelling to Switzerland to see England play and I suppose it was here they were picking up their coaches to the airport.

There seemed to be some sort of scuffle between some flag-carrying Chelsea boys and two or three West Indians who ambled past the pub. Someone told me later that one of the Chelsea lot had knocked the hat off one of the black guys and set fire to it. The blacks ran into some nearby flats. By now we had moved forward and were sitting opposite a little pub. Then they started pouring out from the flats. There were blacks everywhere – in front, behind and from both sides of the road. Some were carrying jerry cans and Molotov cocktails and they were heading straight for the York Tavern! If only mobile phones had been invented – I would have rung the Samaritans. How they marshalled everyone together like this was a miracle without a public address system. And where the petrol bombs came from at such short notice is mystifying, although this was about the time of the Brixton riots. Maybe there was a store somewhere. Their womenfolk were out on the street gripping milk bottles. This looked extremely naughty. Feeling very white, I slithered down my seat a little. The doors of the York burst open and hundreds of Chelsea came screaming into the road. Leroy slithered down his seat a little. Lucky they burst out at that moment; I'm sure a few seconds more and the York would have been torched. Chelsea ran the blacks into the side streets and the flats and thankfully the traffic lurched forward and Leroy and I were away. Riot police, I am told, were soon on the scene and packed the boys off to Switzerland. I don't think anyone from either side was hurt but I truly believe it was a whisker short of being one of the nastiest incidents of football-related violence ever.

One afternoon Sweeney ran a coach to Old Trafford for an evening game. The coach was full to the brim. The mob was beginning to bubble up again. But there was no trouble before or during the game – there very rarely is at United, due to the police having it pretty much sewn up. However, as the coach headed back towards London, it was caught in traffic on the Manchester outskirts and a huge rock came smashing through the window, sending shards of glass all over. The vehicle stopped and the Chelsea boys alighted and looked around for their attackers. Across the road was a pub which soon emptied, leaving a car park full of Mancs taunting the London coach-load. Sweeney's mob ran across the road and followed the fleeing United fans straight back into the pub. The windows went straight in and furniture got chucked around in the ensuing punch-up. Then it was out and back on the coach. It was over almost before it started. Tit for tat. But what no one knew at the time was that an elderly man who had been drinking in the pub had dropped down dead with a heart attack during the mêlée.

A couple of yards down the road, the coach was stopped and everyone was ordered off. People from the pub, who had kicked the whole incident off, were asked to pick out those they recognised as having been involved. Sweeney and a few of the others were arrested and the remainder were fucked off by the police back to London. To my knowledge, no one from

Manchester was arrested, then or later. Once it became apparent that an old man had died during the disturbance, the police threw the book at Sweeney, charging him with manslaughter. He appeared in court but, to everyone's relief, common sense prevailed and he was found not guilty. After that, though, Sweeney took much more of a back seat. Tommy White also got arrested at a friendly match between Glasgow Rangers and Chelsea and was subsequently only seen at the odd game, and soon not at all. Around this time, again at Arsenal, our depleted and leaderless firm ran into Denton. He knew the score and let us pass without incident. I knew him better now. He always played fair. I met him in a café only recently and we laughed and chatted about past hostilities.

With Icky well and truly banged up and Tommy and Kevin out of the way, the Old Bill had finally finished off the Chelsea mob. Or had they?

ELEVEN

Movie Stars

Chelsea's mob did recover, although by the late '80s and the early '90s it was a very different animal from that which had gone before. For obvious reasons, high-profile leaders and rows involving thousands of people were a thing of the past. Clashes inside football grounds, certainly in the top flight, were practically unheard of. But the fighting and the rivalry continued – except that for the first time it really was organised. Although in the '60s, '70s and early '80s there was this popular misconception that football violence was orchestrated, most of the time it was not. The organisation went as far as the mobs being encouraged to turn up and a few faces then attempting to position them as best as they could for the ensuing row, but that was about it. The fighting that did occur was largely spontaneous. Now faces at different clubs were calling each other up on the telephone and arranging 'meets' far from grounds. Encounters with no police presence whatsoever. These clashes happened every week (and still do) and were far more vicious and dangerous than anything that had gone before. To take part in this you really had to be committed. No hangers-on. No faint-hearts riding along for the buzz. This was soccer violence stripped.

Of course, the general public are led to believe that the problem of football hooliganism is no more, the violent tendencies of these subversives being skilfully contained by the crack Football Intelligence Unit. This is the second big football-violence myth. The first was that football hooligans were a mindless minority, something which Joe Public was asked to believe for twenty-odd years. Everyone who went to football knew this to be untrue, at least as far as the minority bit went. And mindless? Violent, unpleasant, criminal – maybe. But mindless? I don't think so. They kept one or two steps ahead of the police throughout, didn't they? And almost anyone who had a mob in football has prospered quite legitimately in later life. Dozens of former top lads run their own successful businesses and some hold directorial office in well-known quoted companies. 'Mindless' does not stand up.

Myth number two claims that soccer violence is dead. Conquered. I am convinced that there has been a collusion between the government, the police, the football authorities and, most importantly, the press to promote this notion. They all have their motives, but the claim is quite simply untrue. The police will point to the decline in arrests at football matches. True, but the violence has been pushed away from soccer grounds. The police get to know about these offs but not until it's too late. A pub has been smashed up and five people hospitalised by the time they arrive. It's not in their interests to talk too much about this trend. The arrests that are making up the statistics are knobheads who shout 'Wanker' at the referee during games. The football authorities will refer to the Nick Hornby generation and point to the fact that girls now feel safe to go to football as illustrations of the sea change that has occurred. And to an extent they are correct. The stadiums belonging to the larger clubs *are* safer places to go to these days, but there are still rucks week in, week out in the lower divisions, even in and around the grounds. These do not get reported nationally, although the regional reporters still write them up. Things have changed.

The bottom line is that since the football trials, the numbers involved in soccer violence have diminished and there is less trouble at football grounds. But those still active in the top gangs are far more effective and dangerous and are staging their clashes away from stadiums. Because first we had Euro 96 and now we harbour hopes about the World Cup in 2006, no one wants you to know about that.

Going back to the turn of the current decade, the police were gung ho. Even though the Hickmott trial was proven to be a farce and similar cases up and down the country collapsed like a pack of cards, they had succeeded in putting the wind up just about everyone. The dawn-raid brigade put away their battering rams and adopted what they thought was a more sophisticated approach to dealing with us. Firstly they began addressing us in mock friendly tones: 'Good afternoon, Mr King. And how are you?' This was supposed to unnerve us, the fact that they knew our names and our faces. But it was the thought of Fulham Old Bill studying scrapbooks and reams and reams of film in order to put a few names to a few faces that unnerved me. What about the good people of Fulham whose houses were getting screwed every few minutes? And, as usual, they had it all wrong. 'Hello, Mr Davis. Haven't seen you for a while.' This certainly succeeded in giving Mr Davis the jitters because he had never been involved in one jot of soccer violence in the quarter of a century he had been going. He was a Chelsea nut who collected programmes and memorabilia. But the law of averages dictated that now and then he was filmed at various grounds standing next to, or exchanging a few words with, some known faces.

It was the video camera that the police considered to be their key weapon. They were like the proverbial kid with a new toy. Cameras had been in the grounds for ages but now the law were carrying hand-held models everywhere they went. They strutted up and down the streets and around the pubs with their beloved Panasonics. At last they had found a deterrent they hoped would be more effective than the good old truncheon. It would be madness to throw a punch with the Old Bill around, so you would make doubly sure you didn't give them the pleasure of filming you performing.

I remember going to Southampton for a game and I'd arranged to meet some of the boys in the city centre. I'd got a lift down there and I headed straight for the boozer we'd said we'd rendezvous at. As I walked to the door of the pub, a policeman stepped forward and shoved a camera straight in my face.

'Leave off!' I remonstrated.

'If you don't like it, we can do it down at the station,' replied the fat sergeant, still screwing up his eye in the lens. That statement must come with the instructions, because all Old Bill use the same stupid phrase every time.

I went into the pub, bought a drink and sat down with the three mates I'd met up with. And there he was again. Fatguts. Standing at the pub window, filming me.

'He wouldn't get away with that in Southall or Brixton,' commented one of my pals.

'Surely it's against civil liberties?' asked my other mate, who had never come across anything like it.

'We ain't got no civil liberties,' I said. 'We're football fans, remember. The scourge of society.'

We finished our drinks and walked towards the ground. Whilst we had been in the pub the cameras must have been breeding, because now there were scores of them being poked into the faces of every Chelsea fan between the ages of fourteen and fifty. Even inside the ground it didn't stop. Standing behind the goal and facing the visiting Chelsea fans was Fatty the film director. All that was missing was a little canvas chair with his name printed on the back.

This continued after the game as we filed quietly past the away supporters' end. I had arranged to meet my friends after the match at Fareham station, which meant catching a train from Southampton, and then from there I would get a lift back to London. My other mates were after the train to Gatwick, from where they would catch a local service home. We were not standing on the same platform as the hundreds of Chelsea fans waiting for the London-bound trains. There had been no trouble all day and Chelsea fans had behaved well. The extraordinarily heavy police presence seemed totally over the top to me. And there he was again, walking towards me with a large piece of black plastic and glass protruding from the side of his face. Roman Polanski with an eating disorder. By now I had had enough.

'Why don't you fuck off? You've taken more than enough film of me today!'

'If you don't like it we can always do it down at the station.'

That was it. I was fuming. I could see a police inspector supervising the departing Chelsea masses on the opposite platform. I crossed over and spoke to him. I explained about the events of the day and how provocative this officer had been. 'There's been no trouble today, as far as I know. Surely this approach is more likely to set it off?' I reasoned.

The inspector remained tight-lipped during my controlled tirade. When I had finished, to my complete surprise, he said he agreed with me entirely.

'Follow me and we'll deal with this now.'

Fuck me, I thought, this is a first – a decent copper at a football match! He approached the sergeant, pointed towards me and began to talk earnestly at him. Fatso went redder and redder, whilst we stood behind the inspector with self-satisfied smiles on our faces. The inspector turned around and walked towards us.

'I really am sorry for the way this officer has behaved. I accept that everything you told me is correct and I can only apologise for his rudeness. I think my colleague has got the message, though.'

He sounded like he meant it and it wasn't just a bit of on-the-job public relations. We all thanked him and the two policemen walked off together. My mate Joe said he even ended up feeling sorry for Fatty, being publicly humiliated like that.

'Bollocks! He was well over the top,' I laughed.

My train had arrived and I jumped on. As it pulled away from the platform, I saw Fatty standing there alone.

'See ya, chunky,' I shouted, to grab his attention. 'Don't forget to do as sir says and behave yourself!'

If looks could kill. I almost choked on the steam coming out of his ears.

But what about all that film? Did anyone really watch it? I hope not. Perhaps there is a warehouse deep in Hampshire where the local constabulary store these films. Reels marked 'Chelsea fan in green jacket enters pub', 'Chelsea fan in green jacket buys drink', 'Chelsea fan in green jacket on railway station' and so on. It wasn't about detection or prevention at all. It was all about harassment. But then the police have always had a disproportionate dislike of football fans. All fans, not just the so-called hooligans, are treated as some moronic tribe who deserve no respect. I know it is their job to prevent trouble and to seek out and apprehend troublemakers at matches, but surely it is not in their remit to provoke trouble? The police in London, at least, seemed happy to co-exist with muggers, burglars and car thieves, but people who have the odd punch-up at a football match, well, that really gets them hot under the collar.

I am reminded of a night game around this time. Millwall were hosting us at the Den. Afterwards the police escorted the bulk of the Chelsea fans to Bermondsey station, where they allowed half of the thousand-odd fans to enter. The other half were pushed back, with the aid of dogs and horses, towards the ground and New Cross station. Here the crowd were met with a double row of police stretched across the road.

'Move on! Keep moving!' shouted the policeman supervising our progress. Somewhat difficult with the wall of police in front of us. The line of blue then decided to charge, on foot and on horseback. The police behind us drove us forward regardless. There was widespread panic. Horses snorted and whinnied loudly. Our main concern was to keep clear of the horses' hind legs, and people fought one another to make sure they did. It was really dodgy. I had been in some bad situations at football in my time but for a few seconds this was life and death. The police had drawn their truncheons and were lashing out at anyone and everyone. Judging by their eyes, they were panicking too. Earlier I had thought the situation had been set up, but now I wasn't so sure. A breakdown in communication, I hope. A kid next to me took the full swipe of a truncheon in the face. He instinctively put his hand to his mouth and found a selection of teeth plopping into his palm. We'd seen the police acting like this, out of control and panicking, abroad, but didn't expect it in south London.

We had somehow ended up on the Old Kent Road, which ran between Millwall's ground and the Elephant and Castle. Things were calming down a bit now. A small mob could be seen gathering further up the road, but in the darkness it was impossible to make out who they were. As we closed in we could tell they had grown from about twenty or thirty to a couple of hundred. The police persisted in pushing us up towards them. Maybe they were another Chelsea firm who had been charged down a side street – or was it some of Millwall's boys waiting to welcome us? Whoever it was, they were staying put, waiting for our arrival.

We'd lost about two hundred of our mob in the mayhem but the ones who were left were all our best faces. Good job too. Before we knew it the roar had gone up and we were engaged in one-to-one combat – two hundred times over. This was Millwall's firm all right, and they were right up for it. Strangely, the police melted into the background; they couldn't have stopped it if they had tried. This was toe-to-toe stuff. At least this lot did not have truncheons or hooves. We pushed them right into the Old Kent Road, where there was room to fight, and we managed to get around them. We were getting the edge, thanks to constant reinforcements arriving in the shape of Chelsea fans still fleeing from the police-inspired riot at New Cross. Their boys at the front were now being over-whelmed by the numbers and decided to throw in the towel and run. As in all rows at football, if your front lot run, your mob is fucked. When the numbers had been equal, the fight could have gone either way. Those Millwall boys would not give an inch, but when they became heavily outnumbered they had to back right off. The police then got around us and marched us the couple of miles back to the Elephant and Castle roundabout, where they slung us on the tube.

Matches between Millwall and Chelsea will always contain the ingredients for trouble. But everything that occurred that day was avoidable. The police literally led us into two full-frontal attacks – one of which came from their own. What is the point of giving away fans escorts back to stations and then allowing only half of them in? Where is the sense in marching the other half to another station thirty minutes' walk away? Especially when that station is being policed by a column of officers who have no idea that this lot are coming and are determined to repel them at all costs. There are two railway stations within a minute of the stadium! And why on earth then march the away fans the three miles or so to the Elephant and Castle, affording ample opportunity for the home fans to have a pop along the route? From a public order point of view it beggars belief.

This series of events went mainly unreported. No one was killed. But they could easily have been. When the horses, police and fans were panicking outside New Cross, I was surprised that no one was. Had someone been trampled to death, it would have been big news. The fans would have been blamed as usual. Maybe the truth would have seeped out. A policeman with a conscience might possibly have told of the cock-ups that had led to the situation. Perhaps some 'respectable' fans caught up in it all might have been listened to. Does this ring a bell? Smacks of Hillsborough to me. The finger of blame for this tragedy was initially pointed squarely at the Liverpool fans, but the families of the dead and injured persisted in forcing the truth out. Now it is looking more and more as if the police were responsible in many ways for the events of that day. I hope they will hold their hands up, but I doubt if they will. As usual they will hide behind their uniforms, and in the event that things do come on top, they will go on the permanent sick.

I'm surprised there haven't been more Hillsboroughs over the years. Football fans were treated like animals and with no respect. And let no one say that this was because some football fans behaved like animals. These conditions, practices and attitudes were in place long before the Dr Marten first tramped the terrace. There is no doubt as to which came first. Now fans are treated with more respect, but not because of any change in attitude from the people who run the game. No, they've managed to tap into some dosh for now. Got to keep the yups happy. Give them proper toilets. Let them drink wine and watch from their windows with panoramic views. But one day, not too far away, the rich will move on, and the clubs will be looking to the ordinary people again for cash. I can almost smell the piss and see the toilets overflowing.

TWELVE

If the Boys Wanna Fight . . .
You'd Better Let 'Em

Chelsea were playing Sheffield Wednesday in the semi-final of the League Cup. It was over two legs, with the first to be held at Stamford Bridge. It was a Sunday game with a midday kick-off and the return was to be the following Wednesday evening. In the home game we lost by three goals to nil in front of a sell-out crowd. For the second leg, Sweeney was running two coaches up to Sheffield, one leaving from Hampton Court, the other from Victoria. Tickets for the game presented no problem, as my mate Stewart was a Wednesday fan who lived a stone's throw from the Hillsborough ground. I told him if he could get the tickets I would double the price he had paid.

'How many, then?' he asked.

'About a hundred,' I replied casually.

'A fucking hundred!' he exclaimed in his broad Yorkshire accent. 'You're tekking the piss. How the fuck can I get you lot a hundred tickets?'

'Well, if you want to earn some dosh, Stewart my old son, you'd better get yer arse in gear and get thinking.'

And he did. Between him, his missus and the neighbours in the street, they managed the hundred. Our day out was on. We had no problem filling the two coaches and everyone had a ticket to get in – each one of them bang in the middle of the Wednesday seats.

Our coach was leaving at nine in the morning and we

arranged to meet the Victoria coach at Watford Gap service station. The coach was impressive. Not the draughty old football specials now – we travelled in style. It was a fifty-two-seater with a video, and as soon as we pulled over Hampton Court bridge a blue film flickered into life on the overhead screen. I don't know why they are known as blue films. They should be called pink films, because that is all you see – shades of pink. As usual, most of us pretended not to be interested. The other coach was similarly luxurious and apparently even had waitress service on board, which lasted all of ten minutes. The poor girl panicked after getting her arse pinched and slapped by almost everyone – and this was before anyone had had a drink. She elected to go and sit next to the driver and declined to serve any drinks. The driver was worried, too; he pulled the coach over and asked whoever was smoking dope to please stop, as he would be tripping himself before he got to Watford Gap. By all accounts, there was so much puffing going on that you couldn't see the front of the coach from the back seats.

As we pulled into the service area, we could see that the Victoria coach had already arrived. The fellas from the second coach surrounded us.

'Where you lot fucking been?' said Cator, who was supervising the Victoria party. 'Stop off at a wine bar, did you? Fucking stockbroker boys.'

I smiled and ignored his banter. He asked me what the plan was. I told him that we should all meet up in Chesterfield and from there catch the train to Sheffield. We arranged to rendezvous at the Chesterfield Hotel, and after most of the lads had stocked up on drink, food and fags, we boarded our respective coaches.

'Don't forget, Mark,' I shouted across to him, 'don't come off the motorway at the Chesterfield exit, come off at the one before. That way we avoid the Old Bill.'

As I slumped into my seat, I remembered going to Sheffield some ten years earlier. There were about ten of us, and with our group that day was a fella called Peter Connelly. Everyone knew him as Puncho. A Millwall fan – I suppose he was their

Icky – he was a great organiser and motivator but also a really good laugh. He could talk his way into or out of anything. As the train pulled into Chesterfield station, Puncho suggested we jump off, have a drink in Chesterfield and then catch a bus to Sheffield. It would make a change and mean less interference from the police. As we stepped on to the platform, Puncho hollered in a faultless British Rail announcer's voice, 'All change, all change! This train terminates here!' With that, everyone left the train. We looked behind us and saw four or five hundred Chelsea fans following us out on to the street. The train chugged out of the station empty except for two transport police leaning out of the window, trying to work out what was happening.

We had a good drink in Chesterfield. I phoned my pal Stewart and he told us the name of a pub near the ground where we could meet him. We took a bus and met up with Stew and drank with him and some of the Wednesday firm for about an hour. You see, it's not all about beating the brains out of one another. That day Stewart was the bridge between us, but there were a number of occasions where we had socialised with other mobs. With some clubs there was a mutual respect. Millwall, despite the vicious offs between us and them over the years, was one club where bonds existed between some of the Chelsea factions and theirs. Puncho, for example, was with us that day.

We left the pub and strolled towards the ground. Stewart pointed out a group of blokes loitering around at the top of the road.

'Those lads ahead are Blades – United fans.' As we got closer he added, 'See the big half-caste lad? He's well-known up here. He's United's top boy.'

We walked straight through the middle of them and they didn't like it one bit, giving us the eyeball.

'What ya looking at, Prick Brains?' challenged Puncho, never shy in coming forward. The big half-caste replied with the usual 'cockney wanker' shit, but they had bottled out – no mistake. We were in their city, we had walked calmly and coolly through their mob and one of us had taken the piss out of their main man. No need for further action at this stage.

More of Stewart's mates came over and he introduced us. We chatted amicably and were surprised to see the Sheffield United boys back again and standing all around us. We looked at one another, knowing what we were all thinking. Let's do it. But who was going to make the first move?

Jerry Kilburn was. He banged one straight in the mouth, and they took a collective step backwards. The Wednesday fans stood shoulder to shoulder with us, and one said to the United firm, 'You fight them, you fight us.' There is no love lost between Wednesday and United fans but this was quite brave, I thought. We'd be gone in a few hours and these blokes had to co-exist with one another in the same city. Also, it was Wednesday playing Chelsea and United thought they were sending their élite squad to give Wednesday a hand against the Chelsea hordes. Despite the Blades' leader trying to shame the Wednesday lads by reminding them that this should be a Yorkshire versus London issue, they stood firm and United drifted off into the crowd. No doubt they would later take their frustration and humiliation out on some innocent young Chelsea boys, but you can't be everywhere at once.

With United gone and Wednesday in truce mode, we elected to have another drink and forget about rucking. Stewart thought we wouldn't get into any pubs around the ground so at my suggestion we decided to try the players' bar for family and friends inside Hillsborough. We walked through the door and were faced with an upright gentleman resplendent in a blazer displaying an array of medals on his chest. He reminded me of the old colonel in *Fawlty Towers*, but not as dotty.

'Yes, chaps. How can I help you?' Before we could answer, he chirped, 'Are you with the Chelsea party?'

'That's right,' said Puncho quickly. 'We're from Chelsea Football Club.'

'How many of you?'

Puncho conducted a quick head count and calculated ten.

'Righto,' said the old boy, 'the free bar is over there, and when you would like something to eat, just take a seat at one of the tables and someone will be along to serve you.'

Stewart was agog.

'I can't believe this. I've been coming for twenty-five years and I've never been in here.'

'Well, you're here now,' laughed Puncho. 'Make the most of it.'

We tried to blend in with the surroundings – not easy – and caned the free bar. We didn't push our luck and attempt to eat, though. After about forty-five minutes we spied the old colonel striding towards us. He was not all smiles now. His cheeks were bright red and his moustache was bristling.

'Right, you lot! Out! Don't bother finishing your drinks. Making a bleeding monkey out of me. Go on – out!'

'What have we done?' we all whined.

'What have you done? I'll tell you what you've done. You've taken the piss out of me.'

He laid his hand on Puncho's forearm.

'How have we?' said Puncho again, in his best injured voice.

'With the Chelsea team indeed!' the old boy snorted.

'Hang on,' Puncho intervened. 'You asked us if we were with the Chelsea party. We obviously misunderstood your meaning. We thought you meant are we Chelsea supporters.'

'Bollocks,' the colonel replied, his already alcohol-tinged face now getting redder and redder. 'Out you go.'

'Thanks a lot, mate.' Puncho shook his arm out of the old man's grip. 'You certainly know how to treat a fellow soldier. Someone who has served Queen and country.'

Colonel Wednesday eyed Puncho up and down.

'I've just finished fifteen years with the British Army,' Puncho elaborated. 'A Northern Ireland stint and just back from the Falklands. I really need this.'

Puncho played the part of the unappreciated soldier back in Civvy Street to a tee.

'What regiment?' asked the old boy, his demeanour notice-ably softening.

'Marines,' replied Puncho, following a crafty look at the old man's badges and tie.

With that his face lit up. He was in the Marines too, he enthused. Puncho and he exchanged some further words, mottoes or something, that convinced the old boy beyond doubt.

'You can stay,' he smiled. 'Keep your heads down and no bother.'

Stewart was impressed.

'You had me going there. I really thought you were in the Marines.'

Puncho smiled.

Today there were two coachloads, so with the best will in the world there would be no chance of getting into the players' bar. As we arrived at the Chesterfield Hotel, Mark's coach was behind. We got off and immediately groups splintered off in different directions.

'Don't forget,' someone shouted, 'everyone meet at 4.30 at the station.'

I wandered off with ten or so others and we took in a few pubs. All afternoon more and more Chelsea fans came drifting into Chesterfield. This town, for some reason, was often selected as a stopping-off point for Chelsea before and after games. There was a general belief among the Chelsea boys that the women were up for it in Chesterfield. Like a lot of football bullshit, I bet it started after a couple of Chelsea boys got lucky one night in the town on the way home from a match, told a few mates and it spread around. It's a bit like Nottingham, where there is said to be three girls to every boy. But women were the last thing on anyone's mind today. Women, even northern ones, don't flirt with mobs of geezers.

Eventually we returned to the station. There were a good few hundred there, most fuelled with drink and champing at the bit.

'Let's go,' urged Cator.

'No, we're not all here yet,' said Sweeney. 'Be patient, my man, and we can all go together.'

In the distance we could see a small army walking towards us.

'Here comes Tony Covelly and his lot,' observed Cator. 'Right, when they get here let's move off.'

Our numbers had swelled to about three or four hundred

and it was all the faces. Every single one liked a good tear-up. This day there were about ten or fifteen factions but we all knew one another well and we all felt confident and secure in the knowledge that this was the cream of the current Chelsea firms. With us was Fat Dave, who had not long been out of the US Navy, Roy and his brother Bruce, Peter Stevens and Brian Wilkes, whom I could trust with my life, Jerry Kilburn, Lane, Justin and Muscles from Tunbridge Wells way – normally to be found on Icky's coaches – and Jeff Paine. Craig and Mark were beside me and I can honestly say I have never seen them take a backwards step in any row. The same goes for Joe and his lot from Crawley. This was a top-notch fighting firm at its peak. We jammed into a Sheffield-bound train, excited and expectant – and we still hadn't seen a copper all day.

At the other end, though, it was different. The Old Bill were waiting and collared the first fifty or so off the train and bussed them straight up to the ground. The rest escaped rapidly into the city centre. They hunted high and low for Wednesday or United fans, but to no avail. During their wanderings they came across a large council estate about a mile from the ground, and hanging about just inside the estate was a group of twenty to thirty Rastafarians. The Chelsea boys crossed the road and walked towards them. The Rastas budged not an inch and seemed to hold no fear. Something made a few of the Chelsea lads look above them. On balcony after balcony they saw row upon row of dreadlocked heads looking down at them. Between the heads balanced along the balcony ledges was a variety of domestic appliances. Chelsea ran straight into the Rastas, who promptly disappeared up some stairs – and the heavens opened.

'Fuck me, it's raining Hotpoint!' screamed one Londoner as dirty old fridges, cookers and tumble driers came hurtling down on to them. Chelsea pursued the Rastas along the balconies and fighting broke out all over. Some of the boys still on the ground were carrying distress flares and rockets and were firing these up into the balconies and into the flats themselves. The sky was alight with Chelsea fireworks. The police arrived with a pack of dogs and literally hunted down Chelsea.

Many were arrested and bundled into police vans. They were held overnight and released in the morning without charge. Seemed like the law were not interested in doing the Rastas any favours.

Those who escaped the great round-up made it to the ground, where we were all pushed and shoved around by Sheffield policemen and their horses. They didn't seem perturbed that we had tickets for Wednesday seats; they were just determined to get us off the street. They rode into crowds of people and attempted to force them through. Parents and children scurried to avoid the snorting horses but the police ignored them. They obviously hadn't learnt any lessons from their disaster of a few years earlier.

'Careful, mate,' I heard one Chelsea fan say. 'You'll have another Hillsborough on your hands. Oh, sorry, this is Hillsborough, isn't it?'

Inside the ground we found our seats and the match kicked off. At half-time we all met up for a chat and a cup of tea. I found Stewart, our covert ticket supplier, and he was well pleased because Chelsea were taking a pounding on the field. A few scuffles were breaking out as we talked but nothing of any consequence, especially considering there were a couple of hundred Chelsea spread out among this Wednesday lot. I went into the toilet for a piss and was just zipping up when I was spun around from behind. Two burly coppers held each of my arms.

'That's him, that's him!' said a young fella, pointing at me. 'He's the one with the knife.'

'What knife?' I said. 'I'm just having a lag.'

Then a bloke standing to my right, who had been watching events, spoke up.

'He hasn't done anything, officer. He has been stood next to me and I followed him in, so I can vouch for him.'

'And who might you be?' sniffed one of the gorillas.

From his pocket the man took out a wallet and unfolded it. I saw the words Doncaster and CID. Fuck me, I thought, another Good Samaritan copper! The uniforms dropped my arms and walked away and the knife fantasist followed them. I thanked the detective.

'That's okay, I knew you hadn't done anything. Besides, we Chelsea supporters have got to look out for one another.'

He explained he was an avid Chelsea fan, having followed them since they beat Leeds in the 1970 cup final. I thanked him again and went and stood at the tea bar. I was telling the boys about my strange experience in the toilets when I was grabbed again, this time by two different coppers.

'Right, son, where's the knife?' one demanded.

'Look, I've just been through this with two of your lot. What's going on?'

'It's all right, officer.'

It was my Doncaster CID guardian angel again. He spoke to the coppers and they too walked off, and then he motioned me away from my mates.

'Look, do yourself a favour, go back to your seat and stay there. For some reason they are on your case and they want to nick you.'

I took his advice but puzzled over the incident for the rest of the game. Was the Doncaster geezer kosher? Who was the civilian saying I had a knife? Very strange. It crossed my mind it was some sort of intricate set-up by Fulham Old Bill. It unsettled me and I never got to the bottom of it. Yorkshireman supporting Chelsea?

Chelsea lost and our Wembley dream was over for another season. We all trudged back to the coach park to locate our transport home. No one spoke.

'It would have been lovely just to get to Wembley,' mused Wilkesy. 'I'd rather lose in the final than in the semis. Well, that's what being a Chelsea fan is all about. Never win fuck all, but the team tease us all season. But we're the most loyal fans in the country.'

The coach journey home was very subdued. About half of our coach were missing in action; apparently the Victoria coach had only ten on it going back. It was a day of anti-climax, both on and off the field. Once we hit the motorway, the overhead video crackled away. Blue films for tired and emotional football thugs. Plenty of climaxes there.

THIRTEEN

Beach Babies

Local derbies. The media love the term. When two neighbouring teams play one another, they are supposed to compete with a fervour and a passion that they apparently don't muster in other games. Manchester City want to beat Manchester United more than any other team, Liverpool–Everton clashes are legendary and so on. All good romance for the John Motsons and sheepskinned radio commentators in building up a fixture. But I'm not sure that this is the case in the modern game. How many Liverpool and Everton players come from Merseyside these days? One? Two? On a pitch chocker with foreigners, why should a local derby be any different for the players from any other game?

But on the terraces it does mean something, and the passion and rivalry are still very much in evidence. Chelsea hate Tottenham, Tottenham hate Arsenal, Arsenal hate Tottenham, West Ham hate Millwall, Palace hate Brighton, Bristol Rovers hate Bristol City, Sheffield Wednesday hate Sheffield United. Basically all clubs have a special hatred for the club which, in most cases, is nearest to them. I have been to all of the big London derbies – Spurs v. Arsenal, Chelsea v. West Ham, QPR v. Fulham, Millwall v. West Ham, Brentford v. Aldershot and many others – and these always seem to spark more trouble than the average game. These fixtures attract local cranks who join up with the hardcore football thugs for the day. West Ham and Millwall especially are notorious for searching across London for each other's mob, even on days when they are not playing one another.

One of the derbies that surprised me most was an FA Cup tie a few years back between Brighton and Hove Albion and non-league Crawley Town. Chelsea had a few boys from Crawley and we decided to travel with them down to Brighton, along with various other mates who were all faces at other London clubs. We had a drink in Brighton and then made our way to the Goldstone Ground. There was no trouble before and during the game that we saw, but we did hear that a two-hundred-strong Crawley mob had been roaming the streets of Brighton before the kick-off. During the match we had to stand among the Brighton fans because the area in the ground allotted to Crawley was full up. It was a big gate, considering the lowly status of the teams, and you could have cut the atmosphere with a knife. I'm sure the Crawley officials were surprised to see they had so many supporters.

After the match ended, about twenty of us decided to walk into the town centre. It was dark, cold and wet, so after a while we hopped on to a passing bus. The bus was empty apart from four young lads sitting at the back. Our little firm consisted of a Millwall fan, two Spurs fans, an Arsenal fan, a West Ham fan and around fifteen Chelsea. On the edge of the town centre the four lads jumped off the bus, being careful to avoid any eye contact with us. A couple of minutes later, Joe happened to glance out of the back window.

'Fucking 'ell – take a look at this!' he exclaimed.

Chasing the bus were a good hundred geezers, shaking their fists up at us like characters out of a cartoon. They looked like Brighton; there was not a familiar face among them.

'They might be Crawley,' said someone, hoping that this might not turn out as bad as it was looking.

'Only one way to find out!' said Ally, one of the two Spurs fans, whilst ringing the bell to stop the bus.

We had begun to pile out when the driver, who had been watching the situation unfold in his rear-view mirror, decided to shut the doors. He was probably worried about the baying mob behind boarding his bus, but all he succeeded in doing was keeping half of us in and condemning the ones who had already jumped off to a severe hiding. We pushed our faces up against the window and cringed as the mob surrounded our mates and punched and kicked them to the ground. It was a fucking free-for-all as the sheer force of a hundred bodies mowed our boys down. We shouted up to the driver.

'Stop this fucking bus now!'

The bus shuddered to a halt and the driver let the rest of us off. Running back towards the action, I could see that one of our lot was lying on the ground in the foetal position. It was Joe, and these bastards were taking turns to boot him. With each kick his body jerked. This was never a good sign. I pushed through the Brighton lot standing in a circle around him, bent down and began to pick him up. Strangely, his attackers didn't go for me and for a few seconds actually made room for me to get Joe upright. All around, the others were exchanging blows with the Brighton front line. Then I heard the sound of a shop window disintegrating. I looked over and saw a Brighton fan lying spark out on the floor of an optician's. One of ours had put him clean through the window. Head first, by the looks of it.

I could see that Brighton wanted to run now but we were not going to give them the chance. They dropped their arms and relaxed their bodies. We spun around and went straight in with the nut, fist and boot. The first few joined their friend on the floor looking up at the stars; the rest behind ran like hares. What a load of shitters! One hundred to ten and they'll have a go. One hundred to twenty and their arsehole goes.

Joe was still a bit unsteady on his feet but thankfully seemed to be okay. As we helped him down the road, Chris noticed that a smaller group of Brighton were standing on a corner looking straight at us. It was dark by now but we could tell that these were not the same wankers who had dished out to us at first.

'Looks like they're back for more,' said Roy.

They sauntered towards us and us towards them. Numbers were about even, so at least they were showing a bit more bottle than the first lot. We stopped with about two yards between us. Their spokesman was a half-caste fella with a large birthmark on his cheek sprouting clumps of hair. Ugly fucker. He fancied himself, though. He thought he was dealing with some Sussex bumpkins who didn't understand what Third Division rucking was all about.

'You Crawley lot fancy your chances, then?' he smarmed.

I wanted to break his jaw now and rip that foliage off his cheek, but I had to tell him who we were.

'Fucking Crawley! We're not fucking Crawley! I'm Chelsea, he's Tottenham,' I said, pointing to Ally, 'he's West Ham and he's Millwall.'

It's not often you introduce your mob individually to the opposing firm, but these sad cases were exceptionally stupid.

'What you doing here, then?' asked tarantula face.

'Yeah, I forgot to mention we're here to bash your fucking brains out.'

My witty words had barely passed my lips when one of theirs nicked a leaf out of our book, stepping forward and cracking my pal Roy on the jaw.

'Martin, Martin!' came a concerned voice from behind me. It was Steve from Tunbridge Wells, better known as Muscles because he didn't have any. He was looking towards a large mob approaching us from behind. It was the first lot we had run, now recovered, walking over to us menacingly.

'And look over there,' added Muscles, never one to look on the bright side. Coming out of a shop on our left was yet another firm, and this lot looked like they had been the first in and first out of the January sales. They were armed to the teeth with carving knives, rolling pins, saucepans, pots and a general array of kitchen implements. As if they didn't have the numbers to do twenty geezers, now they're getting tooled up.

Spiderface smiled at our discomfort and clenched and unclenched his fists in a dramatic way. We were not worried about him but sometimes you just know when you have to have it away. Two hundred geezers are going to smack up twenty geezers, whoever they are. If this were a decent firm it might be worth making a stand. But playing the hero so that these cowboys can tell people for the rest of their lives that they gave Chelsea a hiding, I don't think so. Many years ago Cambridge battered a bunch of Chelsea scarves and they have been dining out on stories about doing Chelsea's main mob ever since.

I looked at Roy and Tony, who were standing with me at the front of our lot.

'Time to go, boys!'

We ran. Through them, instead of away, which shocked them. They gave chase. I didn't look around but I knew they were right behind. I could almost feel their breath on my neck in the cold night air. If you're being chased, though, you either get caught, stop and face it or you get away. You don't just jog around for ages with your pursuers maintaining the same respectable distance behind you. This chase was strictly for ego purposes only. They didn't want to catch us.

Eventually we split up and the chase disintegrated. No one had said anything but we all knew to meet up at the pub we had used before the game. With the exception of Joe, who was still a bit knocked up from his earlier beating, we were all in one piece. All that was dented was our pride. Being slapped about and run by Brighton, even if they had had the numbers, did not look good on the CVs of senior football thugs. But we all convinced each other that having it on our toes had been the right thing to do under the circumstances.

'If we had stayed and had it with them, some of us would have been in intensive care now,' someone said. We all nodded in agreement. But it rankled. We didn't even have a drink in the pub. The blood was boiling. Wished we'd never come.

We find our cars and thread through the evening traffic out of Brighton. Not a lot is said. We feel bad. Feel bad until we clap eyes on the half-chat with the tarantula glued to his face and his mate walking towards us, deep in conversation. We can't fucking believe it! The man who fronted up the Brighton bully crew is dropping straight into our net. They are laughing, and walking with a spring in their step. Probably reliving how they had whacked and legged Chelsea, Millwall and Spurs all over town. They are so excited that they don't notice the five of us in the motor. As they pass we all scratch our heads, covering our faces with our arms, or look down at the floor. We park up and follow them on foot. I can feel that 'payback time' feeling rising in the pit of my stomach. Tony Covelly can barely contain himself. Five on to two. That's the sort of odds Brighton like.

We are on a main road so we can't give them a dig here. Too many civilians about, plus these town centres are all wired up to close-circuit television now. We'll keep following and then give it to them in some backstreet. Preferably in their own front gardens, leaving their wives or mothers to pick up their bits. I look at the others and we're all keyed up. We maintain about a fifty-yard distance and spread across the road, so if they do look behind we don't look as if we're together. There's a sheet of rain anyway, even if they do glance backwards. We're going to savour every moment. It's not often you get revenge. Not this fast.

They turn into a side street and we speed up, but by the time we round the corner they have disappeared. Shit. This is a residential street so they can only have gone into a house. We walk to the bottom of the road and wait. We know they must be in one of the houses near the top of the street, judging by the speed at which they vanished. But if we hang around too near, they'll never come out. Eventually they do reappear, shout something to a man in the window of a house and scoot back out on to the main road. By the time we get out there they are gone. Gutted. We have lost the perfect opportunity for sweet revenge. No qualms. These blokes deserve it and would have been paid out in buckets, and we would all have felt a bit better about what has, all in all, been a bad day.

Joe, who had taken some physical punishment that day, knew some Brighton fans. He asked them to keep their eyes and ears open and let him know who the Brighton firm were. Sure enough, they were soon putting it about locally that they had done a top Chelsea firm who had even been strengthened by faces from West Ham and Millwall. They really thought they had arrived. It transpired that some of their young boys had seen us in the pub before the match and recognised Tony from England games, where he was well known, and me from a Brighton and Millwall match a couple of seasons before.

They had assumed I was a main Millwall face. They had followed us on to the bus, having the foresight to get on at the stop before us after they had seen us waiting down the road. They then alighted near the pub where the main Brighton firm were drinking and tipped them off as to who we were. Hence the Keystone Kops chasing the bus down the road. All of us involved in the Brighton incident resolved that one way or another we would even the score. Brighton had to be taught. And I needed to settle up with the good-looking chap. We didn't make a big thing of it; Chelsea had bigger fish to fry than Brighton. But, for us, we were biding time.

That summer a few of the Chelsea boys decided that a day on the piss down in Brighton was in order, to alleviate the boredom of the close season. At the backs of our minds was the prospect of turning the Brighton boys over and running into you-know-who. Word spread all over about the seaside trip and on the day QPR, Arsenal, Millwall, Glasgow Rangers, FC Cologne and even some Dutch boys turned out for what can only be termed a hooligan convention. Had I known that the day was going to generate such interest, I would have hired the conference centre.

However, if word spreads around the hooligan network like this, you can be sure the Old Bill will be on the case. The meet had been arranged for the big pub opposite the pier. As we crossed the road to enter the place, one of the Dutch lads came running over to us. He urged us not to go inside, saying the place was crawling with Old Bill.

'At half-eleven in the morning! Why? What's happened?'

It seemed that a huge number of lads had been in town early and as soon as the pub had opened its doors at 10.30 they had gone in. The police had turned up in force and had started searching people and arresting them. The Dutch kid knew his tulips, telling us that the police were from the Football Intelligence Unit, supported by Fulham Old Bill and the Sussex Constabulary.

'Marvellous, ain't it?' observed Roy. 'Can't even have a beano to the seaside now.'

Muscles poked his head around the corner. He and some

other Tunbridge Wells lads were keeping their heads down from the police.

'Sweeney and Jeff have just been carted off,' he told us, explaining that the police had allowed everyone into the pub and had then promptly closed it down and started nicking them for fuck knows what. We decided to keep on walking down the promenade. We found a little pub in Hove where we whiled away the day drinking and playing pool. Moleface and his beach babies would have to wait.

The following season Brighton were soon in London, playing at Brentford. A handful of Chelsea and QPR chaps went down there to have a drink with their Brentford pals. The pub they were in got turned over by the Brighton firm and the Brentford boys, along with a couple of Chelsea, got a bit of a slap. That was it. Besides our direct experience with these nonces, stories were coming through about how they had lorded around London after visiting some of the lowly London grounds. A conscious decision was taken, now by the whole Chelsea firm, to remind them who they were and who we were.

We had to wait until the following season for a repeat of the Brentford fixture. It was now getting on for two years since the Crawley row. Our contacts discovered that the seasiders intended to have a drink in a pub in Richmond, from where they were going to catch a train to Kew and walk down to the ground. We plotted ourselves in a pub just down the road in Chiswick. We had some fifty good boys and today were determined to wreak some revenge. Personally, I would have been happy for a toe-to-toe with Spiderman.

Some of our boys were in a car and they had a mosey around, looking for the Brighton mob. We were using mobile phones by now and they would call back to the pub at regular intervals to let us know of their progress. It would have made a good advert for a mobile phone company: who would you most like to have a one-to-one with? After an hour there was still no joy and it was looking as if Brighton had swerved our reception committee yet again. Roy and I jumped in Fat Dave's motor and headed down to a pub at Kew Bridge, hoping we might see them down there. Sure enough we did. Seventy geezers standing outside a pub, drinking. The car cruised up alongside and Roy wound his window down.

'Where you off to, boys?'

The Brighton delegation looked towards us and a couple sauntered over to the motor.

'Who wants to know?' asked an acne-infested young man, peering into the car and looking us up and down. I thought Roy might just wind the window up and trap his spotty head in the car. His mate puffed out his chest and leant against the front wing.

'Who are you, then?'

'Never you mind,' I told them. 'Do yerself a favour an' wait right here, because there is a little firm up the road who are dying to meet you.'

Dave spun the car around and headed back in the direction of our lot, half a mile up the road. We had a quick conference and decided that it would be best to meet in the streets back up towards our pub, where there were no Old Bill. We motored back down the road to reschedule. We got to the pub. They had vanished. Wankers. We guessed they'd headed for the ground and that was where we found them, this time drinking outside a boozer next to Griffin Park. The spotty youth saw us and came over again.

'I thought I told you to wait for us?' said Roy, talking to him as if he were a cross parent talking to a kid.

'We wanna know who you are,' insisted the youth.

Roy shook his head and smiled.

'Look, nothing's gonna happen now. How about after the game?'

'Okay.'

'Victoria all right with you?' enquired Roy, knowing they'd probably be heading back that way anyway.

'Fine. Whereabouts at Victoria?'

'Don't worry about that. You'll find us,' I shouted as we sped off.

We told the others about the arrangement and most of them went off to see Chelsea play at the Bridge, but we made our way straight over to Victoria. I had tried to get a look at Brighton's mob and hadn't seen my friend but I felt sure he would be around somewhere. At about 5.30 a couple of hundred Chelsea turned up. News of the Brighton meet had spread around the seats of Stamford Bridge and everyone and his mother was here. This was an awesome mob, and off the lead too.

'They've got some fucking neck,' mused Roy, 'coming here to meet us.'

'Yeah, but they don't know who they're meeting, remember. They probably think we're a kamikaze little Brentford firm. They've no idea we're Chelsea and they've no idea it's payback time,' I reminded him.

Revenge really is sweet. After a few false starts and eighteen months of patient waiting, the Brighton firm came bowling out of the Victoria main entrance and strode purposefully to the pub across the road. They bounced across the concourse like they owned the fucking place. They had psyched themselves right up and had that 'Come on then, where are you?' walk down to a tee. The pub they came towards was the one we were in. The boozer emptied and we tore into them as if they had gang-raped our sisters. Pure hate. And from the left and the right came two more Chelsea columns who had been lying in wait. The look on their faces was how I imagined condemned men facing a firing squad would look if you whipped off their blindfolds. They were hammered in front of taxi-drivers, shoppers and commuters. They tried to scatter but there was nowhere to go. There was absolutely no attempt to fight back. Self-preservation was the name of the game. Dozens dropped to the concrete, drawing their knees up to their chins to protect their bollocks and their arms framing their heads in the hope of avoiding brain damage. It was truly the worst hiding I have ever seen one mob dish out to another.

A few managed to escape the trap and ran back into the station. Some of us followed, determined to leave no pebble unturned. We found them cowering on trains, begging for mercy. We showed none whatsoever. Some had picked up newspapers from the floor and were doing their best impersonations of Saturday evening commuters. We tore the papers away from their faces, dragged them out on to the platform and pasted them. Back on the concourse, a couple of the Brighton boys snatched up little children and held them in front of their bodies like shields. Some were dazed and walking in circles, crying. Others were lying around the pavement, yelping like dogs. Their cowardice was sickening. I saw a Chelsea boy swing a 'Queue here for taxis' post, which was anchored at the bottom by a lump of concrete, and catch a fleeing Brighton fan full in the back. His eyes were almost resting on his cheeks with the impact but somehow he kept running.

They had been taught a lesson. One they would never forget. They had known that day in Brighton exactly who they were slapping up in the air. It wasn't like they had pasted the wrong people by mistake. They had no brains. That day when they caught us out, they should have just given us a squeeze. A cliché, I know, but they fucked with the big boys and they paid for it big time. Joe later heard from his Brighton mates that some of the firm had been fairly seriously injured and that the Brighton mob, for what they were worth, were well and truly finished afterwards. Really they were nothing. Taking liberties with the likes of Watford, Bournemouth or Torquay – well, that's between them. Hope they have fun. But they were never anything but they made the mistake of thinking they were.

During the massacre – because that was what it was – I had noticed out of the corner of my eye a black taxi pulling away from the rank sharpish. I didn't think about it until afterwards. A photo-image sticks in my mind of a man sunk down in his seat looking frightened and glancing furtively out of the passenger window over an upturned collar. He had dark skin, with an even darker blemish on the cheek. None of us ever saw or heard of him again. Perhaps he's had cosmetic surgery and is living in South America with the pet tarantula he has had removed from his face.

FOURTEEN

All the Fun of the Fair

It's midnight on a cold November night. Fulham Old Bill have just walked away with our passports for inspection, 'to check that everything is in order,' they say. We're in Fat Dave's car, Joe, Muscles, Ginger Bill and myself, waiting to board the 12.30 ferry across to France, from where we will drive down to Vienna. Chelsea are playing Memphis Vienna in the European Cup-Winners' Cup on Thursday night. We've only qualified for the competition because Man U have done the double and as losing FA Cup finalists we're taking their place. Plug, as he is affectionately referred to by all of us because of his resemblance to a character from the *Beano* comic, returns with the passports.

'We have not seen you for a while, Mr King.'

'No. I've not been to football for ten years. I've lost all interest.'

'Where are you off to, then?'

'I'm off on a wine-tasting tour of the Loire valley.'

'So you're not going to the match?'

'What match is that?'

Realising he is not getting any change out of me, he turns his attention to Dave.

'What about you, Mr Kinshott – are you on this wine-tasting expedition too?'

'No, not me. I'm off to EuroDisney.'

He hands back our passports. Eyeing Muscles in the back, he says, 'I know you from somewhere too.'

'Problee,' grins Muscles.

'Okay, on your way, and behave yourself in Vienna,' he says, waving us on to the boat.

Some years had passed now since Hickmott had been banged up and subsequently freed and the relationship between the police and the boys had settled into one of mutual tolerance and grudging respect. It was a mini industry for them. Lots of trips around the country and further afield. Overtime and expenses. Poring over information. Exchanging intelligence with other forces. Basically containing a problem that was really containing itself anyway. I'm sure they loved it. It was in their interests to be seen to be on top of it – but not so much on top of it that the powers that be might consider disbanding the Football Intelligence Unit or any other special divisions altogether. Every now and then an incident would be plastered all over the papers, yet there were similar incidents week in, week out that went unreported.

Ironically, I reckon Fulham Old Bill were quite attached to the Chelsea mob, having spent some years almost living with them. One lunchtime I was sitting on a stool in the Beehive near Flood Street with Mike, a mate from Manchester. Chelsea were playing Manchester United and the Mancs were drinking in a pub up at Sloane Square. Two Old Bill walked in. One, whom we knew, was Fulham and the other was from Manchester. He had the Greater Manchester Constabulary badge on his helmet. The Fulham copper looked around and seemed pleased that anyone who was anyone was in here somewhere. He came over to us at the bar and chatted.

'Hello, Martin. Are you off to the States for the World Cup?' he asked.

'Na, I don't follow England,' I replied, although time would show that England would fail to qualify anyway.

'We're all going,' he went on gleefully, then turning to his colleague from the north of England and adding proudly, 'This is Chelsea's top mob in here.'

The Manchester copper looked around the pub. In these relaxed surroundings, I doubt we looked particularly menacing. I, for example, was wearing a suit, having just knocked off from a morning's work.

'This lot would murder your lot up the road, I reckon,'

continued Fulham. Manchester did not respond and, judging by the puzzled look on his face, I think the last thing he expected was to be engaged by his London colleague in a debate as to who was policing the better mob.

We drove through France, Belgium and Germany, finally arriving in Austria around midday. We stopped in a little village and had some grub before pressing on to Vienna. We hit the capital at about three o'clock and immediately sorted some accommodation, dumped our bags in the rooms and set off to find our fellow countrymen. The game wasn't until the following evening, so we had plenty of time to have a good look around the city.

It didn't take long to discover that many Chelsea fans had already arrived and were drinking in a place called the Swedish Plaza. I mentioned earlier that the reception fans give each other at the beginning of a new season is as if everyone has just got out of jail. Well, all meeting up in a foreign city is like you've just been reprieved from the gallows at the last minute and you've been returned to the bosom of your family. We knew more or less everyone in there and after about a quarter of an hour of shaking hands and slapping backs we realised that, like us, no one had tickets for the game.

Dave went up to get a second drink and asked the barman if he could have his lager in a straight glass rather than the brown clay flagon they had served his first in. The barman took great exception to this reasonable request, despite the fact that we were paying nearly five pounds for a beer the size of a cup of tea and half of that was froth! Perhaps asking for a different glass in Austria is some secret code for 'I want to plate your arsehole'; whatever, the barman came around to our side of the bar, waving his tea towel around furiously.

'Away my bar! Out! Out! Football animals!' he flustered.

He'd obviously read the papers that morning. Dave stepped in front of the barman and just looked at him as he ranted and raved. I knew that look. Here we fucking well go, I thought, Dave's going to plant the nut on Manuel.

Then he said calmly, 'Fuck you. I hope they're not all like you. Fuck the lot of you.'

We walked out to a barrage of abuse about English pigs, the war and Winston Churchill. We were well tired after the marathon drive and decided to turn in for the night.

'That was a strange thing to say about the war and that,' I remarked to Dave as we walked down the road to our bed and breakfast.

'Shows how sad these wankers are. Fifty years on and they're still talking about the Second World fucking War. They can't handle it that they all rolled over for the Krauts and we never. We fucking mullered the Germans and then we had to march around Europe liberating cack like this.'

With a bit of help from the Americans, I thought, but I was gagging for my bed and some shut-eye and so let the political debate tail off into the night air.

The next morning everyone was up for breakfast bright and early. Already there was an old Austrian guy with a bow tie, who looked like a professor or a scientist, sipping his fresh orange juice and studying us over his little glasses that rested halfway down his nose. He was reading a paper which I was sure was full of the Chelsea invasion and dire warnings about what to expect. He carried on watching. Shock! Surprise! They use knives and forks! One taps the shell on his boiled egg with a spoon, ever so gently. And they chat to one another in a quiet, civilised manner. Most strange.

I decided to have a walk around Vienna. Gulping in the crisp morning air, I noticed that even at this early hour there were pockets of Chelsea drifting around all over the place, many with flags draped over their shoulders and Chelsea caps perched on their heads. Not quite the official supporters' club, but not far off. They were holding and folding and looked as if they couldn't wait until the pubs opened. Others walked around in pairs, smartly dressed with no sign of any colours. Not trouble merchants, because I didn't recognise them at all. They had the pinched features and streetwise manner of northerners. I guessed they were from Manchester and were in Vienna for the touting.

The others had said that I should meet them in the bar just around the corner from where we were staying when I had finished playing the tourist. But I didn't fancy going on the piss this early and, being a lazy bastard, decided to go back to bed and nick a couple more hours' sleep. Just as I was dozing off, I felt someone walk into the room and stand by the bed.

'Get up, yer lazy fucker! Is that all you're gonna do all day? Lie in bed?'

I opened my eyes and saw my old workmate Glen looking down at me, laughing.

'Lucky I wasn't having a wank!' I said, more to myself. 'What are you doing here?'

Stupid question.

'Same as you. Watching the Blues and going on the piss with you lot.'

I got dressed.

'I'm meeting the others in a little bar just up the road and then we're going over to the ground to blag some match tickets.'

'How many are you looking for?' asked Glen.

'Well, there's five of us.'

'No problem. I've been over to the ground already and bought six.'

'Glen, you're a fucking star!'

That was Glen all over. Always organised. Always prepared. I bet he was in the boy scouts. Probably still is. Dib dib dob dob. He wasn't one for having a row at football at all. The first sign of trouble and he was off, but when it came to finding a good pub or somewhere decent to eat, Glen was your man. He liked us and we all liked him. There are hundreds of Glens at Chelsea, blokes who love the club and follow them over land and sea (as the song says). Their faces are familiar and welcome. They get on well with the ruckers and we with them. They know what we do and we know what they don't do.

'How did you find me then, Glen?'

'I saw one of your mates walking across the main square and followed him back here. I knew you couldn't be far away. The first door I opened, I looked inside and saw you akip.'

Lucky you didn't barge into the Austrian professor's room in the middle of him mounting his old woman, I mused. Mind you, Glen would probably have offered him a condom.

We went to the bar and the others were well pleased that Glen had sorted the ticket situation. Their eyes glazed over a bit, though, when he started telling them about how he had caught such-and-such an underground and then got a number so-and-so bus. He had our route for later on worked out for us, including which way to run if a fight broke out.

Speaking of fights, we had heard reports from both Arsenal and Spurs fans that the Austrians were game for a row. Apparently when Arsenal had played here they had been bush-whacked walking through a park. The Austrians had come out of the darkness from all sides and it had gone right off, with some of the Gooners taking a right bashing. Spurs, we were told, had come off a bit better but had still found themselves with a fight on their hands. Glen explained that the stadium was in the middle of a park surrounded by woodland. At one end of the park, he mentioned, was a giant funfair. We'd already heard about the funfair. Some locals – in an effort to put the shits up us, I suppose – had told us that that was where their boys meet, and when they see the visiting fans arriving they scurry off into the woods and then ambush them. Yeah, and Nottingham Forest always throw you off the Trent Bridge.

By now our bar was heaving and leaking supporters into the road. The pub opposite was the same. People had been drinking for a long time but there were no signs of trouble. Drinks were being paid for. There was no real singing. Nothing was getting broken. It was about four o'clock and some of the lads were getting restless and wanting to get up to the funfair. Umpteen pints of lager had turned the funfair into some mystical place where you could have the mother of all battles in the dark night air. A familiar face assumed control.

'No. Leave it till half-six. Then we get to the funfair and wait for them to turn up.'

I could see Glen nodding away. He appreciated a bit of organisation, even if it was from a thug.

The authorities had different ideas. It was the riot police with dogs and they were closing all the bars. They pushed everyone out into the street, and only then did I realise that they had rounded up a good thousand or so. A big old mob, but obviously there were a lot of jockeys in there (only along for the ride). The police then formed a line down the middle of us whilst we just looked at them, puzzled, wondering what was going on. They began pointing with their batons, which was their way of telling us they wanted to disperse the crowd. Taking the message on board, about three hundred of us walked off in the direction one of the batons was pointing in, which happened to be towards the underground. The rest were encouraged to head towards the stadium. We filled the platform. Amazingly, no police had elected to come with us. We got on the first train and someone (probably Glen) studied the tube map and worked out that the stop before the stadium would bring us out right by the fairground.

We jumped off there and poured into the street. Someone at the front politely asked a passing couple the way to the funfair. They pointed it out and stood back aghast as column after column of Chelsea fans streamed past. Where have these hundreds upon hundreds of English men come from, they must have been thinking. And aren't they a little bit old to want to go to the funfair? We walked to the top of the road. All you could hear was the sound of marching feet and whispering English voices. Still no Old Wilhelm on our case. Across the main road was the funfair. Getting dark now. Neon lights and organ music.

'Right,' piped up someone at the front, 'if they are in there, let's just take it nice and easy.'

As we crossed the road, I looked behind at the mob we had. I didn't know many of them – there were quite a few youngsters – but they all seemed up for it. You could tell they were just dying to ram some candyfloss right down the first Austrian's gullet.

As we walked through the entrance, we all spotted in the semi-darkness a lot of activity in the trees and bushes ahead of us.

'There's a mob over there,' said someone, pointing.

Out of the shadows emerged about a hundred geezers, and then another hundred, and another. Fuck me! They kept on coming. We were seriously outnumbered. They didn't run at us but they were not hesitant; they simply strolled in our direction. We moved towards them. This is going to be some off, I thought, as I drew in breath. I'm at the front and there's not a sniff of Old Bill. That feeling is hard to describe. I should be able to because it has happened enough times over the years. There's no going back and you know within seconds you're going to be in a right old battle. It's a great feeling. It must be a chemical thing. Nature's way of pumping you up for a confrontation. Cavemen and survival and all that bollocks. Maybe it is this feeling that is the nub of it all. The adrenalin rush of the real risk. You're not to know who you're going to be up against. A maniac with a machete? The biggest, hardest fucker you've ever laid eyes on? Who knows? You know too that your body, your strength and your front have got to overcome theirs if you're going to survive. I've heard people compare this rush to an orgasm. I don't agree, but, like an orgasm, it is impossible to explain precisely what it is about the rush that you enjoy.

On my left they're all laughing. Now they're all shaking hands. Yeah, you don't have to be on *Mastermind* to work out that it was actually the rest of the Chelsea mob from the town centre. There was us thinking that these Austrians were game, and the others were thinking the same!

Now we were all together, the only thing to do was to find the Austrian mob. A couple of boys jumped on a tram and did indeed find our hosts hanging around the ground. They didn't want to know. I'm sure they'd sent some spotters, who had seen the size of our firm and thought, fuck that for a game of soldiers.

We drifted towards the stadium, where there were only two turnstiles open to admit our huge number. Some of the boys got impatient and started pushing, shoving and climbing to make things move a bit quicker. The police were having none of it and began pulling a few people out and arresting them. I dropped out of the swaying mass and let the crowd die down before trying to re-enter. Better to miss a few minutes of the match than risk a nicking in a European city. You'd be on exhibition, with every curious Austrian copper visiting your cell to see how the famous English hooligan reacts to swift baton blows to the softer parts of the body. No thanks. I stood to one side and chatted with Black Willie, Hickmott's mate, and as I did so I couldn't help noticing that a dozen or so police were staring at us intently. One approached and delivered an almighty slap to Black Willie's back.

'Hallo, my good friend. I hope you are not here to cause the trouble.'

Willie slowly turned around to face the Austrian. Now, Willie is a big lump but the slap had knocked the wind right out of him. He had been assaulted for no good reason. Willie squared up to the copper, looking deep into his eyes without blinking. The copper stepped forward and did the same. This was one of the situations in football that crop up now and then. The police challenge you openly, or they do something totally out of order. You know that if you retaliate, you're nicked and banged up for a long time. Nine times out of ten you are rational and walk away from it. Sometimes, however, the emotion of the moment is too great and an almighty riot is kicked off. For a moment I thought it was going to be the one in ten. Willie was in a silent rage. One punch or a good nut would lay out this prat, and I knew the mob we had here could go through the entire force on duty tonight. Then they'd wheel out the army.

'Leave it, Will. It's not worth it. He just wants to nick you,' I said, but they continued to eyeball one another, their noses almost touching. It was obvious that either someone had identified Willie to the Austrian police as a troublemaker or they had looked at him and, drawing on their stereotypes, had reached the same conclusion, and the backslapper had taken it upon himself to show off in front of his colleagues. Someone else had the presence of mind to gently turn Willie's body and guide him away from the stand-off. 'Come on, Will, let's get in the ground.'

The Austrian smiled a sickly smile as if he had won the day. We all knew he was a tosser hiding behind a uniform. And the police wonder why when things go wrong for them – trapped alone in a crowd, or tripped up during a rampage – no mercy is shown. Well, it's because of blokes like that.

We got into the ground and took our seats. The match had already started and as I looked around the stadium I marvelled at the support Chelsea had brought. They were spread across the entire ground and sang their hearts out non-stop. The game ended in a 1–1 draw, with Chelsea going through to the next round on the away-goal rule. And what a goal it was! Little Johnny Spencer picked the ball up in his own half and ran the length of the pitch before sliding the ball into the net. The ground erupted. Once Bates had got him out of the way, Ruud Gullit was accused of doing or not doing a lot of things at Chelsea, but in my book his only crime was to sell little Johnny Spencer much too soon. He is a sweaty, granted, but his heart was in Chelsea just as if he had been born on the Fulham Road.

As the match was ending, it began to look as if we were going to have our fight with the Old Bill, regardless of Black Willie's restraint. They stood in front of the fans, not only around the pitch but at all the exits. They had put on leather gloves and donned riot helmets. The batons were drawn.

'They're gonna have a pop at us, Dave,' I said.

'I think so,' replied Fat Dave, surveying the situation.

Things were going quiet as those who had noticed the police mentally prepared themselves for what lay ahead. I really couldn't work it out. There had been no trouble all day, neither in the town centre nor at the ground. Chelsea had gone through and were in good spirits and there was no home mob hanging around for an off. The Austrians' police advisers from England had obviously omitted to advise them that these were not the ingredients for trouble. The atmosphere was tense, but as we filed out, the police stood erect, looking straight through us like the guards at Buckingham Palace. Common sense prevailed all round.

Outside we hung around on the concourse, waiting to get everyone together. The police were waiting with us, seemingly having wised up a bit, but after a few minutes of watching us chatting, lighting up fags and greeting one another, they got bored and wandered off to stare at someone else.

'The funfair?' someone suggested, and we sneaked off again into the darkness of the park. A tram clattered past.

'I know where you lot are going.'

I looked up in the direction of the voice and there was Glen, hanging out of the tram window.

'Shut yer gob, Glen!'

We smiled at one another. He knew the score. Fuck the fighting; Glen's priority was to find some grub to fill his rumbling belly.

Meanwhile we pressed on through the park, with the strains of 'We'll keep the blue flag flying high' drifting across the night air. The bulk of the Chelsea contingent were in celebratory mood as the police led them down the main road, at least half a mile away from us now. We were back at the funfair in no time. Just as we entered, a police van drove at a snail's pace alongside us. I could see two Fulham Old Bill sitting in the back, no doubt pointing out to their Austrian counterparts the most evil Chelsea thugs. I mean, they couldn't really say 'and there is Punky Al, a real gentleman, follows Chelsea all around the world and has never caused any trouble in his life', could they? Money for old rope. Two-day break in Vienna. Doing fuck all. All at the expense of the British taxpayer. What a life. Makes you wonder who decides that British police officers should be sent out to Austria to watch a football match. No wonder the council tax in Hammersmith and Fulham is so fucking high. The ratepayers are footing the bill for FOBEB (Fulham Old Bill European Beanos).

Having seen those freeloaders in the back of the van, we decided to say goodbye to the fairground and head back to the city centre and the bar where we had been drinking before the game. Looking at Glen, Dave and I suddenly felt hungry and left the inn to grab a pizza. As we moved on from the restaurant, we clocked a small group of youths standing at the top of the escalator which came up from the underground. They were acting a bit strangely, looking to the left and to the right, unsure whether or not to step out on to the street.

'They're Austrian,' I nudged Dave, 'and I bet there's a right old firm waiting at the bottom of the escalator. Look at how they're looking up and down. Looking for us, they are.'

We stopped and stood in a doorway, watching these clowns

in action. They looked like mice looking nervously around to see where the cat was. Pixie and Dixie looking for Jinx the cat. It must have taken all of ten minutes to get their mob assembled on the street at the top of the escalator, and even then there were only about fifty of them.

'When they move, we'll go with them,' I said to Dave.

They headed off towards the bar we were all in, but first they'd have to pass a pub that was packed with celebrating Chelsea fans wearing replica shirts. This was the sort of mob that would have Glen as their leader. The Austrians had just about got past the pub when they were sussed by a couple of Chelsea fans leaving. They shouted something through the door to the inside and the pub emptied. The Austrians were frozen to the spot, not knowing whether to flee or shake every Chelsea fan's hand and convince them they had come in peace. Dave took up the initiative and walked towards the Austrian lot, arms outstretched and wide apart, beckoning them with his hands. This was the traditional posture favoured by English fans who are about to have a row.

For the avoidance of doubt, he growled, 'Come on, then, you Kraut wankers! Who wants some?'

The Austrians looked at Dave and then at one another, puzzled looks creasing their brows. Were they taking the piss?

'Pardon one. I am not understanding the request you are saying,' said one of the Austrians, in all sincerity.

I just pissed myself laughing, and Dave did the same. He couldn't hit the geezer after that. I doubt if any of us had ever come across such a polite fella – especially one we were tensing up to clump. Unfortunately the lot from the pub hadn't witnessed this well-mannered tiff and only saw a stand-off between Chelsea and the Austrians. They tore straight into them and the Austrians ran away as fast as they could as a few fists and boots crossed the language barrier. I was feeling a bit sorry for them, especially Dave's mate, Lord Charles, but they seemed clear away. The Chelsea boys gave up the chase and streamed back into the pub, laughing and joking at the comical little spat. Then a splinter at the back of the fleeing Austrian mob stopped, turned and fired distress-flare rockets straight into us. They weren't that naïve after all. The police must have been watching all along, because at that very moment they steamed straight into us, battering anyone and everyone with their batons.

Back at our less conspicuous bar, we had a good laugh about Dave's confrontation with his European counterpart.

'How did you think he'd understand what "Do you want some?" means? Three-quarters of English people wouldn't understand that!' I ribbed Dave.

'How am I meant to know what to say?'

'"Fucking do you want some?" would have been better.'

'Anyway,' Dave went on, 'he understood some English. He said "pardon" to me, didn't he?'

The following morning we were up and out of Vienna by 7.30 and arrived on the ferry in France by 9 p.m. – and that was after a two-hour unscheduled tour of Brussels after silly bollocks Dave got lost. He was most indignant that the Europeans didn't have the courtesy to write their road signs in English.

On the ferry we bumped into a group of Chelsea fans who had travelled by rail and boat through England and Europe and hadn't paid pound one there or back. We'd seen them outside the ground when they had had to rush to catch their train to Munich. They'd left twelve hours before us and we'd still managed to catch the same boat. They told us how on one train the ticket collector had been fast asleep and they had stuck notes all over him, written from his own ticket pad, saying things like 'Herr Wanker', 'I am an idiot' and 'I am not very good at my job'.

As we drove off the ferry, Plug, the facially challenged Fulham copper, was there again. He leant into the car.

'Good time in Vienna?'

'Yes, very good thanks. Beer a bit on the expensive side, though. Still, that wouldn't have been a problem for your comrades out there.'

'How's that?'

'All goes down on the expense sheet, doesn't it?'

Plug laughed and waved us through. 'Go on, piss off.'

Some time later I happened to be chatting to an Austrian journalist who was in England covering the Wimbledon tennis fortnight. I told him I had visited his country with Chelsea and had enjoyed it. He said that the people of Vienna had been surprised at how well-behaved the Chelsea fans had been. For days beforehand there had been a build-up in the local press about the invasion of the Chelsea Headhunters who were all Combat 18 skinheads bent on destroying their city. The journalist told me that the fears were totally unfounded, everyone was happy and the next time they would welcome the Chelsea fans with open arms. He remarked that he hadn't seen one skinhead all day. Treat people with respect and you will receive respect.

FIFTEEN

Eddie McCreadie's
Blue and White Army

Early 1998. One of the characters mentioned in this book has hit forty and my wife Mandy and I are at the surprise bash. Wild Bill Claridge introduces me to Martin Knight. He's writing a book about the Chelsea gangs, says Bill. I tell Martin that I've done a book and he explains that he was involved in a book but not any more. We agree to exchange a chapter from mine for something he has written. I think it's likely to be the usual tosh because I don't remember him from Chelsea. A couple of days later Martin's bit arrives and it is great. He writes about games that I was at – some featured in this book. He sees things from a different angle from me but reading it is like being transported straight back to the mid 1970s. It is like being there again. Martin rings me.

'I loved it,' he says. 'It's like being there again.'

We agree on lots of things. Especially about the need to get a book out that is authentic.

What follows is the brief account Martin originally sent to me of his days of going to Chelsea in the 1970s.

* * *

There was no real option at school. If you lived where we did, you supported Chelsea. Some kids had their Leeds, Liverpool and Man U duffel bags but if you were serious and actually were going to go, you went to the Bridge. Scrawled on a local bus shelter, clearly in a young girl's handwriting, was the rhyme 'Chelsea boys, Chelsea Shed, Chelsea boys are the best in bed'. That was enough to convince an insecure adolescent of which club he should be following.

I went a couple of times in the early '70s with a friend's dad. I can remember being impressed by the sea of people that was the Shed but I was more interested in the game. The public address system played 'The Liquidator' by Harry J and the All-stars and one by one the Chelsea players acknowledged the Shed's chanting of their name. I just caught the end of the Osgood, Bonetti, Harris and Hudson era. Actually standing in the Shed for the first time was quite an experience. You couldn't see the game but the atmosphere was intoxicating: the singing, the lurching backwards and forwards as one, the delirious celebrations when Chelsea scored. It was like one big jug of beer being swung around by a merry party-goer, the contents going this way and that but the jug never quite spilling the head.

The songs they sang were leftovers from the late '60s and early '70s but specific to Chelsea. Those that stick in my mind include 'His name is Tommy Baldwin', 'I was born under the Chelsea Shed' (to the tune of Lee Marvin's 'Wand'rin' Star'), 'Come on and cheer again, cos Chelsea's here again', 'Tiptoe through the North Bank with a sawn-off shotgun' and 'My old man said be a Chelsea fan', although these humorous numbers were fast being replaced by more direct ditties like 'You're going home in a fucking ambulance'. I especially liked 'Knees up, Mother Brown', when you could recklessly push the people in front of you in the same way as you were being shoved from behind. There was a great kinship and a great sense of fun. Someone in the Shed made up the funniest songs. At least, I *think* Chelsea made them up. You'd hear them in the Shed one Saturday and then you'd hear other fans singing the same thing on *Match of the Day* a couple of weeks later. We used to taunt the northerners with 'You look in the dustbin for something to eat, you find a dead cat and you think it's a treat, in your Liverpool slums'. Who sat down and thought that up? I often wondered.

I don't remember the first game I attended. I know it was the end of the skinhead era. Crops were growing out, it was a sunny day and thousands upon thousands of heavy Ivy brogue shoes clattered on the steps of the Shed end. As if in defiance against a fashion that was slipping away, the whole end sang to the tune of 'The Teddy Bears' Picnic':

> If you go down to the Shed today
> You're sure of a big surprise
> If you go down to the Shed today
> You'll never believe your eyes
> For Jeremy, the Sugar Puff Bear
> Has got some boots and cropped his hair
> And is going to fight for CHELSEA!

I remember big, black John in there. Blackjack. A huge Negro with a shaven head, a lot older than us. He looked like a hard nut; he certainly wasn't afraid of the cold. Come summer or winter, he always wore a sleeveless Levi jacket with nothing on underneath. I don't think he was a fighter but he was Chelsea through and through. I heard a couple of years ago that he died, but I'm not sure if this is Chelsea folklore or fact.

I don't remember much violence, although at the Bridge we sometimes saw scuffles at the North Stand end of the ground which were rapidly quelled by the police. The North Stand boys were older than us and had graduated from the Shed. They ritually attacked any away fans who turned up, but by 1975 only a handful of clubs brought any supporters. Whoever they were, the North Stand used to manage to attack them from the flanks, egged on by the Shed urging, 'North Stand, North Stand, do your job.' One Saturday the Shed got infiltrated. By Bristol City, of all people! City were riding high in the First Division and a few of their boys gained entry to our end. They got in the middle of the Shed and roared up, 'City!' Everyone was astounded. West Ham, or maybe Tottenham, yes, but these yokels, no. There were only a few and they were full of drink. They made no attempt to fight anyone; they just stood there and awaited the inevitable onslaught. A few seconds later they were gone under a hail of fists and boots. The strange thing was that minutes later I saw a few of them being led by the police along the dark walkway at the back of the Shed and they were relatively unscathed. Seven or eight guys attacked by hundreds and no real damage. That was quite often the case. Perhaps that gave me the courage to enter other clubs' ends not so long after.

One Boxing Day, though, it all got a bit too close for comfort. We were playing West Ham and the Shed was heaving about an hour before kick-off. Something was different: I didn't recognise the faces and the average age seemed more like twenty-one than the usual sixteen. Suddenly masses of claret and blue scarves were brandished from inside coats and cardigans and the refrain of 'We're forever blowing bubbles' rang out. To a man, Chelsea ran to the outer edges of the Shed. I headed towards the comforting line of police behind the goal. I had just witnessed my first end being taken, and I didn't like it.

Soon I started to go to the London derbies. One Arsenal game sticks in my mind, although I'm not sure what year it was. You go to these grounds so many times, the incidents all blur into one. Because Arsenal were a big club, a bigger club than Chelsea, I expected the seniority to be repeated on the terraces. Especially on their territory. We got in the North Bank no problem. I was down at the front looking up at the end and I thought I recognised a few faces. I saw this muscular chap, not far from me, with one sleeve of his green army-style jumper tied in a knot. He either had his arm in a sling or he only had one arm. At the time a one-armed guy with the strength of three men was part of the Chelsea legend. We'd all talked about him at school and in the snack bars at the back of the Shed but none of us had ever seen him. It was always 'So-and-so saw him do this' and 'So-and-so saw him do that'. I felt sure this was him. I knew it was him. It was like spotting a rare bird; you spend years looking at pictures of, say, a buzzard in books, and then one day on holiday in Devon you see one! I caught the man's eye and felt scared, hurriedly pulling my programme from my pocket and pretending to read. He turned and threaded his way upwards into the centre of the North Bank, with five or six equally fierce-looking men following. There was still some time to go before kick-off and the atmosphere was electric.

'It's going to go off,' I said. It did. All hell was let loose. Arsenal were running for their lives, panicking, heading this way and then that way, pulling each other back and climbing over one another in their fear. My heart was pounding and my stomach was churning –

and I was only watching! Chelsea formed a group in the middle of the end, darting out here and there to shoo off any Arsenal who had the audacity not to run. The police came flying in and surrounded the Chelsea fans. There were too many to eject or lead across the pitch to their rightful end, so they contained them in the North Bank. Arsenal's famous end. With a fat blue line between them and Chelsea, Arsenal began to make half-hearted attempts to get at the infiltrators, but for me that was it. I had to get as much of this as possible.

Not long after this I went to my first away game outside of London. The venue was Luton. This was a different world. The Chelsea hordes had gathered at St Pancras for the short trip north, swigging from beer cans, singing, shouting and swearing. They outnumbered all other travellers by ten to one. There was a carnival atmosphere, a feeling that there would be no one to fight but one way or another they would have some fun. One of the trains in front of us was set alight and ours was completely wrecked. They even made up a song about it: 'Chelsea sing, Chelsea fight, Chelsea set the train alight.'

Once in Luton it was obvious that the police were unprepared for this mobile crime wave as the Chelsea mob rampaged to the ground. I don't recall the score but Chelsea were losing. There was a row with some stewards; I think they had hauled a young kid from the crowd and knocked him around a bit. Suddenly, like a dam bursting, the Chelsea crowd from behind the goal were on the pitch. So was I. Chelsea were on both sides too and they came on from there as well. The Luton goalkeeper was attacked and the players left the pitch. I remember big Micky Droy literally throwing some fans back on to the terraces. Anarchy. A hot-dog seller in his white coat brandishing a bread knife, surrounded by Chelsea after his takings. On the pitch lording it. The feeling of power.

Slowly the police regained control and the game continued. The pitch invasion was nothing, though, compared to what happened in the town afterwards. Luton was demolished. The Luftwaffe couldn't have done a better job. One Chelsea lad entertained us all by kicking in the window of a bed shop and mounting the plastic dummy lying in one of their display beds. Broken glass littered the streets, and shoppers and residents fled in terror. This was vandalism and rebellion on a scale I never thought I would experience first-hand. By the time we got back into London it was headline news in evening papers and on TV bulletins. The town officials were estimating the damage bill to be hundreds of thousands of pounds. Pictures of a burnt-out train dominated the Sunday press. We were the famous, the famous Chelsea. To cap it all, my mate Tony Jones, who had started going to Chelsea at the same time as me, was pictured in a Sunday national on the Kenilworth Road pitch, in flight, with a policeman tearing at his T-shirt.

We revelled in the notoriety and relived the thrill as often as we could. No one had been hurt physically, at least not that we had seen, so there was no conscience to wrestle with. Luton changed me. This was the first time I had experienced the thrill and power of being a mob. Never again would I stand in the relative safety and tranquillity of the Shed. This was the attraction for me at this stage, and for many others, I'm sure. Vandalism was a favourite pastime of many teenagers. To be able to indulge in it on such a scale and in such an open and public manner was beyond a dream. We were also at the age when the police were a natural enemy. Back home in the suburbs they had the upper hand; they could slap you about and then nick you for D and D and there was nothing you could do. But at a football match, or at Chelsea at least, the odds were a bit better. Sometimes you might be lucky enough to sneak a crafty boot in the kidneys of a frightened copper as he waded into a hostile crowd.

When big clubs got relegated from the First Division, they terrorised the Second Division, it seemed. Manchester United re-established their hooligan credentials the year they dropped down a division in the early '70s. West Ham and Tottenham repeated the trend to a lesser degree but, not long after Man U's escapades, Chelsea made it an art form. There was a sort of Millwall 'No one likes us, we don't care' mentality around at the time. An 'Our once-great team is shit but we don't give a shit', 'Our team won't leave a mark but we will' sort of attitude. The fans were certainly more famous than the team; sometimes, I swear, it was the team watching the fans and not vice versa.

That first season in the Second Division we were taking more away than we had done for a long time in the First, with almost as many travelling as attended a home game. The police had not learnt the Manchester lesson and in many cases were incapable of dealing with these weekend invasions. Many of the original Shed boys were now hitting their mid to late twenties, as the average age of the Chelsea mobs climbed. Millwall's firm were always older and until now Chelsea had had a bit of a 'mouthy teenager' reputation. By the mid 1980s, when the Chelsea gangs were headed by a variety of thirtysomethings, Millwall's top boys must have been ancient. Police infiltrating them could have done worse than hang outside Bermondsey post offices on pension day. As the Chelsea boys got older and wiser together, they became more of a fighting force to be reckoned with. Sure, there were still hordes of spotty youths itching to kick your windows in or turn your car over, but at the core was a dangerous, effective mob.

Some time after the Luton beano I travelled up north for the first time on the football special with a group of other nineteen-year-olds. About halfway through the journey, Eccles, then the undisputed leader of the Chelsea mobs, pulled back the sliding door and entered our carriage. He was then a man of thirtyish, with neatly cut black hair and sideboards. He wore a green army jacket, pressed cords and plain lace-up leather shoes.

'You lot rucking?' he asked.

He was accompanied by two nasty-looking lieutenants who were looking us up and down for traces of insecurity. We all nodded agreement.

'I don't mind if you're not, but if you are, do as I say and don't run or you'll have me to answer to.'

To our amazement and amusement, he pulled from his pocket a crudely drawn diagram entitled 'Bolton End'. I remember it had arrows pointing to hot-dog stalls and other such landmarks. His instructions were for us to walk to the Bolton end in pairs or singly and attempt entry; if we failed, we were to walk around the ground and try again until we were successful. He even told us the names of some local towns and villages we could pretend we hailed from if quizzed. He also suggested, jokingly I think, that we practise our northern accents. Once in the ground we must make our way to as close to the centre of the covered area as we could manage, he told us, and join in the Bolton chants until we heard him roar 'CHELSEA!'. At that point we were to lash out at the Bolton fans around us. Then, when they had run (which he assured us they would), we were to regroup as a tight, compact unit. His little speech was tinged with a hint of self-mockery. However, he continued down the train, issuing his instructions, and within a couple of hours I was forced to revise any scepticism I had.

Before the journey was over, though, he was back in our carriage. Peter Bromley and Terry Leonard had an argument which ended with the two of them trading punches and the weight of their crashing bodies smashing the carriage window. Some onlookers in the corridor fetched Eccles. This time he turned up in our carriage with Babs and Greenaway. For a young Chelsea apprentice, this was like having the Beatles turn up in your front room.

'What is going on?' he demanded, looking frighteningly cross. He told us that we should save our fighting for the game. Greenaway whispered something in his ear. 'You'll have to pay for the window. We'll have to give British Rail a tenner for that,' he said and held his hand out. We dutifully dug into our pockets and produced two pounds each. He smiled as if to say everything was okay now. When they went, we all bollocked Brom and Terry, for their little scrap had depleted our spending money by half.

We gained entry to the Bolton end on our first attempt and obediently made our way to the centre. Suddenly I realised what a dangerous situation I was in. This was a big, big end, with hundreds of fuming Boltonians as far as the eye could see. They were singing songs about hating cockneys and surging backwards and forwards. I noticed they had homemade tattoos on their hands, something you didn't see too much of at home. I prayed we were not the only ones who had got in! As we neared the middle I recognised some faces from the train, and there seemed to be a lot of winking and nodding going on. Still, I was not convinced and was about to hedge my bets by moving to the front, closer to the police patrolling the pitch, when, during a lull in Bolton's singing, a throaty roar of 'CHELSEA!' rang through the air. All hell broke loose as Chelsea fanned out, boots and fists flying. As the man had said, Bolton ran and the end was taken. Within seconds the police had formed a cordon around us and we spent the rest of the game teasing the deposed northerners. They were seething when they looked up at us and realised that perhaps as few as five hundred Chelsea had taken an end five thousand strong.

After the game Eccles took us what he called 'walkabout'. He shook off the police by sending a decoy mob one way, leaving us to roam the streets looking for Bolton fans. I think they had seen enough, for there was no one around. The highlight for me was when he led us up a grassy bank and suddenly two hundred of us were on the motorway. I got the feeling he had done this before. To the amazement of the motorists who had to stop, he took us across and then back again. The Grand Old Duke of York.

'General' Eccles made a real impression on me. I remember hearing his name as a first year at senior school, therefore by 1969 he was already a bit of a folk hero in football's urban mythology. His name was daubed in paint on a wall by the Nell Gwynn on the King's Road for years and years. To meet him and, indeed, see him in action was like meeting an England player or a pop star. He was certainly charismatic and had a huge devoted following. After that Bolton game he walked the length of the train collecting 'contributions' from all of us for fines. The notion that the donations would go towards anyone's fines was a bit far-fetched but no one argued. He sat down having collected probably fifty pence from each of the five hundred or so on the train.

'That'll pay for the Canaries in the close season,' he smiled as he sat down with one of his deputies. There was always a little gaggle of followers with him. They got his seat ready on the special. Dealt his playing cards for him. Told him who was and who wasn't on the train. It really was like the king and his courtiers. After one game where Chelsea had met some serious resistance (I think it was Forest), I remember him walking down the train congratulating his troops, sympathising with the injured and generally raising morale. That Forest game was a violent affair. For some reason the police decided to give us their end, which saved us taking it but incensed the Nottingham boys no end. Our friend Willie dived into some Forest fans in the enclosure, got nicked and drew three months on his first offence.

Greenaway was the other big celebrity leader of the era. His name was probably more famous than Eccles's. He had certainly been around longer. I never saw him partaking in any fisticuffs, but he still commanded great respect and because of his legend was obliged to be surrounded by tough lads to prevent attack from less understanding opposing supporters. His cry of 'Zigger Zagger' was well known the country over and a great comfort to cells of Chelsea fans alone in big, cold, northern grounds. Long before the days of all-seater stadiums, Greenaway and his entourage sat down. I have a vivid memory of his arriving just after kick-off at some god-forsaken ground and making his way to his seat. Chelsea had filled this particular stand and they stood in unison and gave him a standing ovation. There were confused looks from the pitch and other parts of the ground. Was it Peter Osgood? Sir Richard Attenborough? No, it was Mr Zigger Zagger himself.

But Eccles was where the action was and I was hooked. At West Bromwich Albion some weeks after the Bolton episode, I made his acquaintance. My friend Kevin Merchant and I had gone to buy a hot dog about fifteen minutes before the end of the match. Milling around the stall was Eccles and about thirty other lads between twenty-five and thirty years old. He assumed we were joining their rendezvous. That had not been the intention. He said the idea was to go down to the home end and attack the West Brom fans as they came out of their end. I thought about the inequality of numbers and, as if reading my mind, he said, 'We batter the early birds and we disappear.'

Again, it happened just as the man said. As pockets of unaware West Brom fans left the ground, they were faced with a snarling bunch of about fifty or sixty Chelsea. This lot didn't muck around, punching and kicking anyone who looked remotely like one of their firm. But before we knew it the big gates had opened and West Brom in their fullness poured out. Heavily outnumbered, we ran on to the wasteland which connected the ground to Smethwick Rolfe Street station.

'Link arms and form a circle!' barked Eccles. I was standing next to him and he linked his arm with mine. There was no going back now. My heart was pounding but I didn't feel scared. We stopped and formed the circle. 'Don't break the link and they can't penetrate us,' he commanded. Pinching a chant from the Grunwick labour dispute which was on our TV news at the time, we roared, 'We're

Chelsea, united, we've never been defeated.' The West Brom mob, whose members were mainly black, were visibly unnerved by these actions. We stepped towards them. They turned and ran.

Back at the station, we were drunk on success. Babs had been battling somewhere else with his little team and Eccles recounted the incident to him. He turned to me to support his story.

'How many of them were there?' he demanded.

'About five hundred.'

'How many of us?'

'About fifty,' I replied.

'What happened?'

'They ran.'

He smiled and patted me on the back. The great man had acknowledged me.

On the train on the way home, he was buzzing. 'You gotta get fitter,' he chided some of the boys around him. 'You're out of shape. You should join the Territorials.' Everyone laughed. 'No, I'm deadly serious. The TA will get you in shape and you'll love it.' He was serious, too. There he was, London's most famous football warrior, recruiting for the Territorial Army. That was the problem for him: he was a soldier without a war.

A night game at Sheffield United. My pal Kevin decided to kick a bus as we came off the train and got nicked immediately; the rest of us found Eccles and his entourage as we walked to the ground. He remembered me from West Brom and was happy for us to tag along. There was no attempt to get in their end this time. I don't know why. I wondered who made these decisions and how they were communicated to the troops. I wouldn't like to be in the group who automatically tried to enter the United end and, whoops, no one else in there. But it never seemed to happen like that.

At the end of the match it was pitch black and we were spewed out on to the Sheffield streets. The police were herding us, not very gently, back to the station, where the special awaited us. One group suddenly did a left into a *Coronation Street* side road and then the next group swerved off to the right and so on. The body of fans being escorted to the station was thinning out all the way but the police hadn't noticed. As if by magic, about four or five different packs met up a few streets away. All walked purposefully, collars up to protect them from the night wind. The command 'Ssssh' was regularly issued when voices were raised, especially when one idiot attempted to kick off a Chelsea chant. Eccles was at the front, walking fast, the mob copying his pace.

'Left here . . . slow down . . . keep the noise down.'

He was in conference with a man beside him who was wearing a beret. I think he called him Sean. They were trying to work out a route that would bring them face to face with the departing United fans. Then, in the still of the night, we heard the sound of their mob. It is hard to describe. It's more of a feeling. The sound of lots of feet gently pounding the roads and lowered voices hanging in the air. Rolling. Then, suddenly, they were there in front of us. They must have lost their escort too. They were close enough for us to see their numbers but we couldn't see the whites of their eyes. Time stood still. I found myself in the front line again, a confrontation imminent. I was frightened and excited at the same time. There was no question of running. This was much more personal than Bolton. No possibility of losing yourself in the crowd. No police to hide behind.

We started to walk towards them and them us. Oh my God, they're not going to bottle! The walking broke into running and then a charge, complete with Zulu-type war cries. Within seconds we were among each other.

'Stop, stop, stop!' people were screaming.

'It's Chelsea!'

'We're Chelsea!'

Laughter all round. A few bruises for some but the story on the special home was how Chelsea had taken on Chelsea in the backstreets of Sheffield. No one had run and it was good for morale.

I always thought Babs's mob was more violent than Eccles's. Eccles was the General, totally committed, but I always felt it was a game for him, as if he was practising for something else. Most of the time we ran up and down the streets or got chased up and down the streets. Taking ends was his speciality but on most occasions he executed it so well that it was painless for both sides. I don't think he had hate in him and, rightly or wrongly, I felt safer with him. Others who started going around the same time as me soon moved on to follow Babs, but my instincts were to tag along behind Eccles.

I witnessed a touch of friction between the two main men once at Plymouth. We had got in Plymouth's end at about 2 p.m. and there was no resistance. This was a piece of piss. We were junior boys and had taken their patch whilst the real Chelsea lingered over their drinks in the pub. So we thought. Minutes before kick-off the terrace started to fill and hundreds upon hundreds of red-cheeked men were all around us. Some wore tweed jackets and round glasses. They looked more like the left-wing relief teachers they used to bus into our comprehensive school in the early '70s than football thugs. But they were in West Country bitter overdrive and they steamed into us with a real vengeance. We fought back and held our ground for a while but their numbers kept increasing. Not entirely discredited, we were bundled out of the end.

Eccles was not at all happy. Chelsea had been hammered and he had not even been able to give an account of himself. He decided to use the 'steaming the end when the gates open for the early leavers' tactic. A few of us still smarting from the humiliation joined him as he strolled calmly down the side of the ground. He looked back and weighed up the thirty or forty soldiers and would-be soldiers behind him. He was unsure. Plymouth had shown them-selves to be game and he was not about to embarrass Chelsea further. He alighted on me.

'Go back and tell Babs to bring a firm and follow us in.'

This seemed like good logic. I ran back to the Chelsea-designated end, tapped Babs on the shoulder and said sheepishly, 'Eccles says could you bring a few and, er, follow him into the Plymouth end?'

Babs laughed.

'If he wants to play the hero, let him play the hero,' he replied, and made no move from the spot. Unsure what to do next, I just stood there and watched. Seconds later the end exploded as Eccles and the boys ran them all over. Babs shook his head admiringly and smiled. The rest of the end roared appreciatively. Pure theatre. Job done. Reputation intact.

On the way back to the station we had to run the gauntlet. Across some playing fields on a hill, Plymouth lined up to throw bricks at us. We could do nothing. The police flanked us on both sides but made no attempt to stop the missile-throwing bumpkins. Eccles, not one to risk a nicking, kept striding forward. As the bricks rained down, he screamed, 'Head 'em back, head 'em back,' and in true Peter Osgood style he rose and met a house brick with his forehead. Blood striped his face but he kept walking.

For some reason I was with Babs's mob when they took Molineux, home of Wolverhampton Wanderers. I'm not sure Eccles would have attempted this. I think he liked to succeed and if he thought the odds were against him he'd leave it. He was pragmatic. That day, though, the power of Babs's mob was apparent, because Wolves fought back viciously against this ultimate humiliation. But these blokes were up for it.

It was on the morning of that Wolves game that an incident occurred that upset me at the time and sticks in my mind now. We had bunked the trains on the Friday night. It was the early hours of the morning and day was breaking. Groups of us were huddled in shop doorways, grabbing some sleep or killing time before the greasy spoons opened. A man in his early thirties came walking purposefully along, a sandwich box clasped under his arm. He was obviously heading for work. He was whistling and seemed oblivious to scores of prostrate young men lying all over. One Chelsea boy barged him for no reason but the man kept walking. The same boy, now looking a bit stupid, caught up with him and punched him hard on the side of the head.

'Northern bastard!'

The man swung around.

'What was that for?' – but he tailed off as he saw about twenty youths in the shop doorways start to stir and move towards him. He turned around and tried to walk away but his nightmare had only just begun. A young man in a sheepskin coat who was sitting up against a shop window tripped him as he attempted to hurry away. He was not running, not because he didn't want to provoke a chase but because he had dignity. He fell and like hyenas ten or so boys and young men were on him. The worker valiantly fought back against his attackers and they were all shaken by his ferocity and brute strength. At one point I thought he was going to do the lot of them. I say 'them' because my pal Mick Woodham and I had no part in the attack. We were guilty, though, of doing nothing to stop it. And we could have done; most of this little gathering were even younger than us.

Eventually the man succumbed to the odds. He adopted the foetal position and just jerked as boots and shoes thumped every part of his exposed body. Mick and I urged them to leave him alone, saying he had taken enough. We picked him up and were glad to see that he was conscious. He was covered in blood but he brushed himself down, picked up his sandwich box – which was empty, the contents having spilled out, squashed and smeared with his blood, across the pavement – and walked off. I felt like crying for him. Minutes before he had set off for his factory job, like he had done every morning for probably nearly twenty years, without a care in the world except perhaps the fear of redundancy. And then he is pounced upon and beaten like a dog by a gang of strangers, almost on his own doorstep.

My guilt trip was rudely interrupted. He was back. He hurled his sandwich box to the floor, clenched his fists and screamed, through his tears and blood, 'My watch! My watch! Give me back my fucking watch!'

No one replied. Some looked at the floor, some looked away and others pretended to be still asleep.

'It was a present from me mam. She's dead now. So give me my fucking watch,' he cried, like an animal in pain, fixing his stare on a big chap who had been one of his assailants. The Chelsea boy knew the guy meant business. He turned to a smaller boy, the boy who had delivered the first punch.

'Give him his watch, Barry,' he said.

Barry tried to smile but no one was laughing. He took the watch from his pocket and threw it at the man.

'Wanker,' said Barry.

The man picked up his watch, put it on and continued on to work. None of us was in any doubt as to who the wanker really was.

I think it was the same season we played Hereford United. Hereford against Chelsea. Only a couple of years earlier such a fixture would have been unthinkable. Hereford were a non-league club and Chelsea were a First Division glamour side. But Chelsea had fallen and Hereford had risen. To the Second Division. We went in Clive Aldridge's Ford Transit, about ten of us from Epsom. Driving through the night, all Clive could offer was one tape to play on the eight-track. Rod Stewart. I must have listened to 'The Killing of Georgie' about twenty times on that journey. Homosexuals were rare then, or at least songs about them were, and although I felt sympathy for Georgie's plight on first hearing the song, I was soon wishing that the New Jersey gang had taken him out earlier.

On our arrival, we pulled into a big pub car park. The owner came hurrying out towards us as we started to climb out through the back doors. He took Chris Mallows as our leader.

'Sorry, you can't come in here,' he apologised.

'And why is that?' asked Chris as he wound down the window.

The publican was not for explaining.

'I think you dropped this,' he said to Chris, proffering a twenty-pound note.

'Certainly did,' smiled Chris, plucking the note from his hand. 'Come on, boys, off we go.'

Twenty pounds! That was phenomenal. Some of us weren't earning a great deal more than that a week. I suggested that someone else should drive and we should go back there in about half an hour to see if he pays us off again, but even Chris knew that that would be pushing it a bit too far.

The ground was different gear. They might have been in the Second Division of the Football League but the stadium, if you could call it that, was only a notch above Isthmian League. Weeds sprouted out of the terraces, you could gob from the top of the end and reach the pitch and there was absolutely no segregation. There was no need that day, though. There was absolutely no Hereford. After the game, Chelsea rampaged. I seem to remember charging through a cattle market, frightening the animals. Chris delighted in all this hooliganism. 'Over with the cars!' he roared. And the Chelsea boys obediently surrounded a new Morris Marina and rocked it until it toppled on to its side. Walking towards us was a throwback from the '50s. He was a young man in his early twenties or late teens. He was covered from head to foot in badges, a Hereford scarf was wrapped tightly around his neck and a massive rosette was pinned to his chest. Beneath his bobble hat he wore a huge smile. No one had told this bloke that things had changed a bit. It hadn't occurred to him that he might be in danger. Why should it?

'There he is,' shouted Chris, pointing at the guy, 'the leader of the Hereford!'

Chris was joking. Football was one big laugh for him, but the mob who had just turned over a car at his request were too stupid to realise. Chris walked on, having probably already forgotten the throwaway remark, but behind him a gang of Chelsea boys had literally pummelled this poor fellow to the ground and were taking penalties with his head. Tony Jones and I looked at each other in horror. This was not on. We shouted at them to leave him alone and pushed through to try and pick him up. The idiots ran off to catch up with Chris for some more fun and Tony and I helped the Hereford lad to his feet. There was no point. His body was limp. His eyes were closed and blood pumped from his mouth in time, it seemed, with his pulse. He was in a terrible way. A silent crowd had gathered and I thought he was going to die. Suddenly I didn't like this football lark, and I'm sure Tony felt the same. Eventually an ambulance turned up. The ambulancemen jumped out and, bending down, lifted his eyelids, but his eyeballs were not there. They took his pulse and lifted him on to a stretcher. I was relieved they didn't put the blanket over his head like in the films.

'What happened?' asked one of the ambulancemen.

Tony and I stayed silent.

'The Chelsea lot just jumped on him,' said a boy in the crowd.

They turned to us. One was red with rage.

'I bet it was you cunts.'

We shook our heads.

'You're scum, you lot from London,' he went on. 'That boy is mental, you know.'

The biggest end I ever witnessed the taking of was the famous Holte End at Aston Villa. This was a team effort and planned well in advance. Obviously if the police had been infiltrating the gangs in those days, it would have been tumbled. Employing the same tactics as at Bolton, every Chelsea fan attempted entry either singly or in pairs. Me and my pal Terry Knowles got in okay but a lump came to our throats once we were inside. This was like the Kop at Liverpool. Much, much bigger than Bolton. Villa fans were loud and there were thousands of them. The worry must have shown on our faces, because we were soon approached by a young Villa fan who asked us the time. That old chestnut. The game was up. We smiled and shrugged our shoulders and he scurried back into the throng, presumably to alert the lads.

Our legs were like jelly as we awaited the inevitable onslaught. There was Villa in front of us, behind us and next to us. No edging towards the police for safety was possible. We saw the young boy in conference with some older lads, pointing down at us. It must have been nerves, but Terry and I just started laughing. But fate intervened. Higher up in the end, the roar of 'Chelsea!' went up and the whole end exploded. No one was bothered about us any more. Firstly Villa surged upwards to attack these impostors. But Chelsea were unbelievably well organised, leading simultaneous assaults from four or five different directions. Villa scurried past us and we kicked and punched them as they ran for their lives, the same blokes who had been going to do that to us seconds earlier.

That was a violent day. There were further clashes outside the ground and a mosque was attacked by Chelsea fans. That was the first time I really noticed the racial thing creeping in. I heard later that a man had nearly died in a brawl in a mosque and that a top Chelsea face had been charged with attempted murder. My friend Peter was West Indian and I could see he was beginning to feel uncomfortable. He stopped going completely a couple of seasons later. I didn't like it. Peter had the Chelsea lion tattooed on his black arm and had stood side by side with the best of them for Chelsea. Yet he had been driven out. Even some of his old schoolfriends, now heavily steeped in the new Chelsea culture, blanked him.

Blackpool was a screamer. We left Epsom in Clive's new Escort van when the pubs shut. A geezer from our own pub did our back windscreen with a machete as we left the pub car park. This was a domestic argument between a local hard nut and Big Dave, who was in our party. Not a good start. Crammed into the back of the van, for a reason that escapes me, was Bruce, the Doberman pet of Chris, who was a bit of a ringleader at Chelsea in those days (Chris, not the dog). We reached the seaside town at daybreak, hung over, miserable and deprived of sleep. None of us had really grasped just how far it was.

We wandered the Golden Mile and were soon re-invigorated as we met up with pockets of similarly bedraggled Chelsea fans. Within an hour we were one hundred strong and making our presence known. An Indian man wearing a turban stumbled into us and was jostled. I thought he would just make it past us when one lad unleashed a ferocious punch to his head. He fell to the ground and his turban unravelled. I was surprised to see his long, flowing hair. Back then there were very few Indians around, at least down our way. I remember a season or two earlier, at Leicester, being shocked when buying fish and chips from Indians. Little did I know that twenty years later I would be shocked to be served in a newsagent's by an Englishman. I think it was Napoleon who said that England was a nation of shopkeepers; were he alive today he would probably observe that England is a nation of Asian shop-keepers.

We moved into an amusement arcade. It was empty save a few men feeding one-armed bandits. Big Dave started to shake his machine with both hands and was approached by one of the men.

'Stop that!' he said.

'Fuck off, unless you want your nose broken!' was Dave's rather direct retort.

The man, surprisingly, pointed to the bridge of his nose and smiled, 'Right there.'

Dave swung his head back as if to head a football and butted the man full on. Within seconds three similarly dressed men were on him. Arms up his back and feet on his face.

'You're nicked!' snivelled the first man through a stream of blood running from his nose into his mouth, brandishing his ID. They frog-marched him away and the rest of us dispersed sharpish. I doubt if it was yet 10 a.m. and things were not looking good. To this day I have never seen Big Dave again. He got three years for GBH on a police officer and served his sentence in Walton nick, from where he wrote to a few of us in the early months of his bird. When he came out he settled in Leeds but soon ran into problems there and ended up back in the nick. He was well known at Chelsea as a big lad who could have a fight but, as the policeman incident demon-strated, he was a bit of a psychopath and you never knew when he might turn on you.

We moved on to a large pub on a hill and started the dinnertime drinking session. The pub soon filled up with Chelsea. Fuelled by lager, we quickly fell into table-thumping, foot-stomping Chelsea songs.

A lad ran into the pub and shouted, 'Man U at the bus station!' As one we burst out of the bar and charged like demented animals into the bus station. The idiot was right. Man U were in there – two of them. Trainspotters, civilians, barely in their teens. We turned when we saw the absolute fear in their faces but some wankers still threw their pint glasses in the boys' direction, causing a couple of Emily Nugents to huddle together in fear as their Saturday morning shopping trip turned into a nightmare. Back in the pub, another small firm from Epsom had arrived, having travelled up on the early-morning InterCity. We greeted each other like long-lost relatives with bags of hugs and back-slapping – which was strange, considering that we had played pool with most of them some forty-eight hours previously! They had walked through the town and said that the place was teeming with Jocks. Apparently it was 'Scottish weekend' in Blackpool, an annual ritual where the whole of Glasgow decamps to this English seaside town for a drunken binge. That promised to put a slightly different complexion on proceedings.

We got to the ground early, about 1.30, and fifty or sixty of us gained entry into their end. Actually it was all one end but split into two. There was hardly anyone in there and we lolled around in ones and twos, chatting and reading the programme. The end steadily filled with locals but no one seemed to suss us. A Chelsea special arrived and suddenly there were a thousand cockneys screaming and abusing us through the fence. Some gave us knowing smiles.

Chris was our most senior member and I suppose he decided now was the best time to act, while we still had a chance numbers-wise. He moved to the centre of the end and roared, 'Blackpool!' The locals, none the wiser, quickly rallied around him. He then rolled out 'Maybe it's because I'm a Blackpooler, that I love Blackpool town'. Predictably, this confused the northerners for a bit, but then the penny dropped – especially as we were laughing at their puzzlement. They began to shape up to us and we ran down at them. They scattered down the terrace to an appreciative roar from our friends in the south, but we were heavily outnumbered and were under attack from behind. All the time more and more Blackpool were pouring in and things suddenly looked very bad. Our boys were only feet away but could not help us, as they were securely penned in. We turned and ran back at our assailants behind. This time they did not run. This gave the first lot courage and they ran us back up the terrace. Somehow we ran through them in our determination to get out of the end. Boots and fists bounced off our heads and legs as we fought our way to the top of the terrace and literally scrambled down a mud bank to the turnstiles. The police, who had not been in evidence on the terrace, stood by the turnstiles, arms folded and smiling. We screamed for them to open the gates and let us out.

'You made your beds, now lie in them,' chuckled one.

For what was probably a few seconds but seemed like an age, they allowed the Blackpool mob to batter us as we tumbled on to one another, protecting our heads from the blows. Finally they let us out and pushed us into the next-door terrace. We sort of expected a hero's welcome (not sure why, because we hadn't put up much of a show) but things had moved on. The Scottish contingent was now in on the act, Rangers fans teaming up with Blackpool and Celtic with us. This doesn't marry up with the special relationship that Rangers and Chelsea are supposed to have, but that's how it was on that day. David Hay, an ex-Celtic player, was in our team, so perhaps that was the reason.

Both ends were heaving and raw aggression charged the atmosphere. Two fences with a wall of police in between were all that separated the two factions. People started to drop around me as we were showered with coins, masonry, bottles and glasses. Clive, our driver, fell to the floor, blood pissing from his head. We went to pick him up.

'Get up, you woman!' shouted Eccles, who was practically orgasmic on the excitement.

Clive didn't; he really was hurt. A couple of policemen fought their way through to us and carried him off. I was beginning to think it was safer on the other side of the fence.

'You're going home in a fucking ambulance,' we roared, and then . . . nothing. I was going somewhere in a fucking ambulance. A cider bottle had knocked me out; at least, it was brown glass the nurse picked out of my head at the hospital. I remember being helped into an ambulance but nothing before. There were two blokes already in there. One was Chelsea and had a nasty cut over his eye, the other was lying down and being tended to by the ambulancemen. He had Blackpool's colours on but he had not been the victim of a vicious attack. His appendix had burst, and he was screaming and writhing in agony. Watching and listening to him, I felt quite fortunate.

The hospital was like a war zone. The ambulances were delivering the injured by the dozen and a couple of nurses briefly inspected our injuries and put most of us into a queue. Some more serious cases were led or carried off to another part of the building. Hostilities were on hold as Blackpool, Rangers, Celtic and Chelsea fans alike queued like good British people for their stitches. My friend from the ambulance and myself were a long way down the line.

'Fuck all this,' he said. 'I only came up here for the minge.'

He kept looking at his watch. Then, without warning, he just crumpled on the floor. A couple of nurses ran over, picked him up and led him away. Five minutes later he was walking past me, out of the hospital, with five or six nice stitches over one eye. He winked at me, with his good eye, as he left. I was becoming concerned too; the match would have finished and I was wondering if the others would go without me. I waited what I thought was a respectable time and then pretended to faint. No one came to pick me up and I had to get up and brush myself down looking a right prat.

After about an hour I finally got stitched up. There was no ambulance to take me back to the ground and I had to catch a bus. I felt quite exposed; there were groups of Blackpool hanging around the streets but no Chelsea. The specials would have left ages ago. I was on my own and they could spot me as easily as I could them. That was something that always baffled me, because even in the '80s, when the firms all wore the same gear, you could tell the northerners a mile off and they could tell us. It must have been their hair, or the way they walked, or their complexion. I don't know.

I found the car park where we had left the van and there was a bit of a stand-off going on. Our van was practically the last motor on this bit of wasteland and about fifteen Blackpool lads were standing threateningly by the exit. Our lads, about seven strong, were leaning against the van. Chris spotted me and could see I was hesitating about walking past them. He opened the back door of the van, pulled Bruce the Doberman out by his choker and walked menacingly towards the lads. The others followed behind. Bruce played the part beautifully, straining at the leash and foaming at the mouth. They didn't run but they walked off at quite a pace. We all jumped in the van and got out of that fucking town. Clive and I, who were both nursing sore heads and fresh stitches, had to share the driving on the long journey home.

The next generation of leaders started to come through. Greenaway was a figurehead, Eccles was too well known and too clever to get nicked – by the early '80s he had withdrawn almost completely – and Babs, for whatever reason, was around less often. Icky took up the mantle and over the next six or seven years established himself as the most celebrated hooligan of all time. He was a very articulate and funny man who oozed charisma. Most people liked him but his style was different again from what had gone before. Not for him the glory of taking an end; he wanted the buzz of a definite confrontation and invariably got it. Millwall were called 'the bushwhackers', but Icky's mob were masters at turning up at unexpected places at unexpected times and confronting unsuspecting mobs. People went with Icky because they knew it would happen.

Chelsea had loads of little mobs, though. The notion that one or two leaders ran Chelsea was always a false one. Slough had a firm, so did Tunbridge Wells, so did Hillingdon, so did Reading, so did Woking, Swindon and so on. We all did our own things; very rarely was it organised in the way the media presented. Chelsea took six thousand away on occasion – how could any one man organise that lot? There were a lot of famous faces at Chelsea, agreed, more than at any other club, I fancy, but they didn't always have the respect of all the firms. Some made a point of keeping away from the faces, as they tended to attract hangers-on and, latterly, the attention of the police.

Years later my mate Paul Hearne and I escaped from Butlin's in Prestatyn, where we were on holiday with our wives and young families, to visit Old Trafford for a hostile evening clash. We were penned in our rightful end – this was the '80s and the taking of ends had gone out of fashion. Thousands of Mancs in the seats above us were raining coins and saliva down on us. I think we were winning; we quite often got a result up there. They were mad for it. I felt quite uncomfortable seeing the hate in their bloodshot northern eyes. But we had to stand there and take it.

It was close to the end of the game and I was worrying about how to get back to the motor in one piece when a huge cheer went up from the Chelsea end. The Man U fans above us were struck speechless. At the opposite end of the ground, the world-renowned Stretford End, the home fans were running. Like Arsenal, all those years before, every which way. Chelsea were in there and were running them. We jumped up and down and roared; we turned around and laughed at the dumbfounded Manchester fans surrounding us. Who that Chelsea firm were, I don't know. It only lasted a couple of minutes before Man U regrouped and, with the help of the police, firmly expelled them. I heard later that there had only been about thirty Chelsea and they had stormed the end when the gates were opened for the early leavers. It was a massive piss-take rather than a serious attempt to take the end but it was sweet. Manchester United fans have rewritten history since and tried to pretend this never happened. But I was there and so were 40,000 others.

I am nostalgic about those times. I miss the excitement and the laughs, but most of all I miss the camaraderie. Friendships formed in those times were good ones. In 1976 we played York City in the FA Cup and Chelsea invaded this lovely old city. We arrived in the early hours of the morning, having caught the InterCity after a night on the piss in London. It was like visiting another continent. Although it was January, it had been fairly mild when we left Euston. I was wearing only Levis and a sad American cavalry shirt which even had sergeants' stripes on the sleeves. As we got out at York, the snow was thick on the ground and it was biting.

We managed to hang about on the stationary trains until the city began to wake up. For some reason, when the shops opened we stormed Woolworth's and nicked the entire supply of plastic Viking helmets and swords – I think this was Bromley's idea; I would have preferred to have raided a shop full of warm clothes – and then staged a mock battle on the city walls. As we chucked each other down the steep, snowy banks, a bemused crowd gathered. They were laughing and clapping at our antics. Mind you, when we tried to find a pub it was a different matter. Most of them had notices up saying 'ON POLICE ADVICE THESE PREMISES WILL NOT OPEN AT LUNCHTIME'. By now there were hordes of Chelsea who had reached York under their own steam roaming around the streets. John Taylor, who was really a Cockney Red but had come up with us for the crack, spied a little pub called the Golden Fleece. He went in alone and had a word. In a few minutes he came out.

'It's sweet. Just us lot.'

We followed him down a long corridor and entered a back bar which was half full of local lads and men. There were about twenty of us and they watched us enter cautiously. Third pint in and we were all the best of friends. Most were not going to the game; some said they followed Leeds. One of the Yorkies alighted on me and insisted I tell him about all the famous fights I had been in. After my sixth pint I didn't know I had been in so many. I found it hard to take him seriously as he had streaming tears tattooed down his face. As we left to walk to the ground, the landlord, who must have taken a right few quid, said we were all right to come back after the game if we liked. Bring a few mates.

I can't remember the score. I spent the entire game sleeping off the lunchtime session, but somehow we had the energy to return to our little pub. This time there were about fifty of us. The same locals were in there but now they had their mates, families and girlfriends with them to have a gawp at this strange Chelsea race. The girls were all over us and the blokes didn't seem to mind. Being a cockney (from Epsom?) and a Chelsea fan made us attractive to these girls and as the night wore on some of us were quite successful in the bunty stakes. The blokes were all over us too. They assumed that because we were Chelsea we were hard and accorded us an automatic respect that we didn't deserve. They took us out around the town and showed us off to all and sundry. We went in a big bar called the Painted Wagon and were the centre of attention. I got chatting to a nice young girl and decided to stay with her when the main crowd moved on to a night-club called the

Old World. After a while it became obvious that although she was interested, she was not that interested, and I left her to find the night-club. Outside in the night air I was on my own, but no matter. We'd taken over York, hadn't we? And York had made us their guests.

Two youths pulled up on a motorbike. One kept the engine going and stayed on the saddle whilst the other walked over to me as he unfastened his crash helmet. 'You Chelsea, mate?' Even through the alcohol I knew what was coming next. I shrugged my shoulders and smiled. He spun around with his arm fully outstretched and hit me full on the side of the head with the crash helmet. It knocked me down and he could have really given me a kicking, but he ran back to the bike, jumped on the back and roared off. I went back to the Golden Fleece and found that some of the boys had also drifted back there. The guvnor announced that he was going to bed and locked up the till. He put a cereal bowl on the bar and told us to help ourselves but to put our money in the bowl. He said that when we had had enough we could doss down on the seats or floor. Such trust. Such kindness.

We made some friendships that night in York that still exist today. One of the lads married a Yorkie and we carried on visiting in smaller numbers for many years. Ironically, though, it was at York, many years later, that I experienced my most frightening encounter with soccer violence. About five or six of us had gone up for the weekend to stay with our friends Marcus and Nick and have a couple of days on the piss. We'd all more or less stopped going to football by this time and were busy working and raising families. One of the Yorkies suggested we go and watch the match that afternoon. York were hosting Millwall and we agreed to take a stroll down to the ground. Millwall had about five hundred in the ground and York, as usual, had no boys to speak of. We were standing in an enclosure at half-time when the Millwall lot got close up to the fence and started to try and antagonise the York fans individually. The Yorkies ignored them. Steve Fisher, who was one of our crowd, eventually bit.

'We ain't York,' he said through the fence, 'we're Chelsea and we're up here for a sort-out with you divvy cunts.'

Thanks a lot, Steve. Hearing his accent, they believed what he had told them. I have never seen a mob get so excited so quickly. Suddenly a boring little day trip to York had become quite interesting for these nutters. They charged at the fence and shook it furiously. The fence looked pretty secure and, what the hell, Steve had said what he had said, so we threw the abuse back at them. A lot of York fans, not really understanding the situation, gathered around us and this Millwall lot really believed there was a Chelsea firm up here just for a row with them. The police had picked up on the excitement and, in their laid-back, no-nonsense Yorkshire way, came and ushered us away from the fence. I was relieved to be led away from this confrontational situation but felt a bit unnerved by the way the Millwall fans were all making throat-slitting gestures at us. Sensibly, so we thought, we left the game ten minutes before the end, chuckling over how we had wound the Millwall boys up and how they thought there was a tidy Chelsea firm travelling two hundred miles to a game they were not involved in just to have a fight with them. We were not chuckling for long. From around the corner appeared three young men.

'Come on then, Chelsea, it's just us,' the half-caste one said, beckoning us around the corner from which they had appeared. Steve stepped forward and launched him into space. It was one of the quickest and hardest uppercuts I have ever witnessed. His two mates screamed out and from around the corner stampeded the hundred or so lads we should have guessed would have been waiting there. I suppose there were about fifteen of us and I knew we didn't stand a chance. I ran for my life, thinking the others would do the same. Most of them did, but Steve backed himself up against a *Coronation Street*-type front door and started putting them down as they came at him. It seemed he floored about five before he succumbed to the sheer numbers. I was like a hurdler as I ran down the road, jumping the Millwall feet as they threw their legs out to trip me. I don't know why but when I saw a little Paki shop I ran in, jumped the counter and ended up in the middle of the family's sitting-room. The football results were on the telly and standing there taking them in was Nicky, our host from York. He had had the same idea as me and beaten me to it. We could hear the shopkeeper screaming at the Millwall fans pouring into the shop.

'Don't worry,' whispered Nick. 'Follow me out the back here.'

He led me into a labyrinth of red-brick alleys and eventually back to the house he shared with his older brother Marcus. It was like walking on to the set of *Emergency Ward 10*. Marcus had the witch hazel and bandages out as he attended to the various injuries suffered by our party as they individually reappeared at the house. Terry Knowles had been battered with a roadworks sign and Steve had taken a bad kicking to his back and legs. He was coughing up blood in the kitchen and that night couldn't really drink, which was a bad sign. Some of the Yorkies had taken the worst of it and were nursing broken noses and badly cut and bruised faces. It could have been a lot worse, though. We had wound up one of the top firms in the country and Steve had really laid out one of their main boys. We could have been knifed, or worse.

The next season we all turned up for a big Millwall cup game at the Bridge. There was bad trouble that night in the streets around the ground. Steve bumped into one of the first three Millwall fans to have come around the corner the year before.

'Remember me?'

I have found that there is a sort of loose old-boys network that exists – freemasons with scars and tattoos, if you like. You meet old Chelsea boys all over and in all walks of life, and those shared experiences give you a bond. I am not ashamed of anything at all. Football hooliganism has a stigma. But most young working-class males went through it, to different degrees and for varying lengths of time. Mods and rockers fighting on the beach at Margate, does that stir up widespread condemnation? Not these days. Most people involved would admit to that. This is now looked upon as a quaint '60s phenomenon. Domestic football hooliganism of the 1970s was not very different.

I packed up in the early '80s. No specific reason. I got married, I didn't like the race thing (although I thought it would pass), I grew out of it. Good job I did. The police, for all their undercover operations and infiltration, still didn't have much idea and ended up locking up as many innocent people as they did guilty. If you were there, it could have been you.

SIXTEEN

The End?

I've been in or around trouble at football for over thirty years now and I'm still hearing and reading about what could or should be done to eradicate the problem. I'm amazed that, after all this time, it excites people so and they still search for a solution and a cause. Do they really want to solve the problem, I wonder?

I can see how it has been allowed to get to this stage, though. There was a huge outcry after that Spurs versus Chelsea match back in 1968 – although that was by no means the first serious outbreak of trouble at a game – yet nothing was really done. A few fines and bans. As my old man used to say, the quicker you put out a fire, the less damage there will be. Instead it was allowed to grow and a whole culture was permitted to develop whereby certain clubs and certain characters became modern-day working-class heroes whose legends spread across the country. Before they knew it, soccer violence was a national pastime. Open to all. Easy to join. Easy to leave. Five minutes of fame beckoning. People make rational decisions as a rule and the pros for young men looking for excitement outweighed the cons. Pros: a fight, a chase, respect from peer groups, male bonding, a laugh, the nearest to a slice of anarchy you can get anywhere, a dig at authority and so on. Cons: the occasional slap, the odd fine. No contest. Not until the Government altered that balance would they stand a chance of tackling the problem. By the time they did, it was no longer a fashion, it was a way of life, and dishing out bird to a few well-known faces could not wash that away in a few weeks.

As the phenomenon built, the hooligans were nearly always a few steps ahead of the police and the football authorities. It took them an age to get their heads around basic segregation and even longer to comprehend that there were two types of young people attending football matches: troublemakers and non-troublemakers. Even now, less-clued-up forces have difficulty spotting the difference. Then, probably most importantly, there was the publicity thing. It took twenty years before it dawned on someone somewhere that the gangs thrived on publicity. The more you wrote and broadcast about it, the more the firms performed. Every mob wanted to see their exploits in print and they wanted other mobs to see it too. Reputation was everything. Take that away, the 'oxygen of publicity', I think they call it, and you are halfway there.

The mid to late '80s were the quietest I can remember, inside and outside the stadiums. Football firms were dying off. Even the top clubs who used to be able to pull up five or six hundred boys were reduced to about half that. Of course, there was still trouble, but only a select group of people got to hear about it: the hooligans, the police and the witnesses. All-seater stadiums played their part too. You can't mob up very effectively in seats. Not only did the new stadiums keep the hardcore firms apart, they also kept them from coming altogether. Even if they did group, they would be picked up and filmed for the duration by the closed-circuit television. It's not that a sudden leap in technology facilitated the successful fight against violence in soccer grounds. CCTV has been around for years. The logic of all-seater stadiums has been around even longer, and so has the money. It was the will that was missing. No serious effort was being put in.

Long gone are the days when you could charge across the pitch to attack the fans at the opposite end of the ground. Sometimes mobs would climb out of their end for one massive punch-up in the middle of the field. Most of the time it was mass posturing, though. You'd turn back halfway and pretend you were only having a laugh. They might do the same, or, as was the case at Bolton one year, you'd pass one another on the pitch and literally swap ends. Don't tell me the crowds (the rest of them) didn't love all this, because they did. That was half the fun of going to football in the earlier days, watching the rucks. There was no real danger of getting smacked up if you didn't want to, whether you were wearing the club's colours or not. Firms, as a rule, only fight other firms. Everyone else is generally left alone. Women, children and families are not attacked at football matches. There were a few instances in the very early days, I think. Leeds once beat up a Man City dad with his kid, and Chelsea were guilty of some pretty stupid bullying and vandalism in their early-'70s marauding days, but the rules of engagements were soon made clear and adhered to.

I laugh at the silly measures brought in over the years to combat football trouble. It makes you wonder about the basic intelligence of those responsible for these initiatives. They never went to the fans and tried to find out what it was all about, how it worked. I mean, taking the laces out of people's boots! Confiscating the actual footwear if they were steel-toe-capped! Can you imagine the manpower involved in that? Hundreds of policemen bending down and unlacing thousands upon thousands of Dr Marten boots up and down the country every Saturday. Someone had been reading too much Richard Allen, and even he freely admitted that he'd never been to a football match! Then they banned rattles, flagpoles, steel combs, bottles and cans, alcoholic drinks and swearing. Chelsea, as usual, had to go one better. Uncle Ken announced plans to erect an electric fence around the perimeter of the pitch. That's it, Ken, fry the boys in bobble hats running on to the pitch to pat Kerry Dixon on the back! Such was the media-inspired hysteria of the time that his plan was considered as a serious proposal.

'The hooligan element'. That is what we were called. 'Hooligans'. The Houlihans were an Irish family who caused a lot of grief around south London in the last century, so I am led to believe, and the name slipped into the national language. To my mind, a 'hooligan' was what your teacher called you when you carved your name into the desk with a penknife: 'You young hooligan, King!' Someone who causes damage to property, vandalising phone boxes, smashing windows, scratching cars and kicking bus shelters. To me, it doesn't describe someone who has a punch-up at a football match, unless that someone is ripping out seats for ammunition.

All those things you associate with young people, boredom and towns. And in towns every weekend there is drunkenness, bad language and fighting. You get nicked and on Monday morning you're up in front of the magistrate for D and D or disturbing the peace. You're bound over or fined twenty pounds. Do the same thing in the vicinity of a football stadium and you are a football hooligan. A monster. A threat to the very fabric of our society. It is all bollocks, and most people know it. When the press decided to lay off the whole soccer violence thing for a while, they looked elsewhere. And they found the very Friday and Saturday night thing I'm talking about: the drunken violence of young men in every town, village and city that has been happening for centuries. They rechristened them 'lager louts'. It's hard to believe it now, but for a couple of summers the press had us believe that lager louts were rampaging across middle England, kicking to death vicars during sermons and gang-raping women's bowling teams on the village green. Never underestimate the role the papers play in all of this. They obviously believe that the masses need a demon festering amongst them (they may be right) – teddy boys, skinheads, punks, lager louts, football hooligans, joy-riders, drug addicts – and they pump it up for all it's worth. Fuck the consequences.

As I'm sure you've gathered by now, I believe that the police's role in the whole thing has to be examined. Most of the coppers I came across over thirty years were decent and fair people. It is not them I'm having a dig at. My point is that the whole police/football thing has become institutionalised. There was no grand plan. It just has. Going back to the Saturday night brawl outside the Dog and Duck, you end up in court and are fined twenty pounds. Same offence at football and you cop five hundred or a grand. Think about it. Who was paying for that mass policing at matches? The clubs paid in part, but the rest must have come from the court coffers one way or another. Most games are at weekends, so a lot of the police will be on overtime. Time and a half. Maybe double. Plus it's not hard work. Not really dangerous. There are a couple of hundred coppers on duty and there are no arrests. Where is the money going to come from? Who is going to carry on forking out? They had to nick people just to keep the gravy train going, I reckon. To keep the dosh coming in for the policing in the first place. We've all spoken to coppers over the years who have admitted they wanted trouble to continue because they got the chance to watch their favourite team and get paid overtime rates for doing so. It was a game. They knew it and we knew it, but apparently no one else did.

It is a bit different now. Clubs have wised up to the fact that the police were taking the piss and have started employing stewards, bringing in the police just for the nasty games or a bit of back-up here and there. The uniformed police have had to reluctantly accept that the gravy train has finally stopped after a quarter of a century – but the big boys still cling on. There is a Football Intelligence Unit, for Christ's sake. Are there really people employed full-time on this? Now? It seems there are. How many, I don't know. How much it costs the taxpayer, I don't know. Someone should ask, because I bet it is not cheap. They are laughing chocolate biscuits, I'm telling you. A bit of effective policing at crucial games controls all these days. Perhaps setting up a unit for international tournaments only could be justified, but that's about it. The hooligan has been successfully diverted away from the stadium here at home, and international matches are few and far between.

But the mobs still exist and they still have it with one another on their own terms at pre-selected venues. Football hooligans are criminals, so the police tell us. Hooligans are fighting hooligans, therefore criminals are fighting criminals. Rarely is there any damage to property. The cost of hooligan activity is minimal to the taxpayer. The police are here to protect decent society. Or so I thought. So why the disproportionate effort to stymie criminals having the odd tear-up with other criminals? There have to be other reasons. The police have been having a laugh. Successive Home Secretaries have fallen for it, and so have the media and the public.

And now there is a whole industry writing about it. Essentially it is a nostalgia trip. I think the fact that there is such a demand for these books supports the assertion I made earlier that football hooliganism was not a minority thing. Most young working-class men in the period between 1968 and 1988 experienced it to some degree, and although many will not admit it now, they loved it. It was a heightened part of their lives, like shagging birds in the backs of cars or driving motors too fast. It was part of their youth.

Very few books, I think, do justice to the subject of football hooliganism. The first crop that came out were written by academics, university boffins who studied it from a sociological and political viewpoint. I'm not sure they really got anywhere or said very much. They still subscribed to the theory regarding links with unemployment and poverty, which was always crap. Then some American professor wrote *Among the Thugs*, which was considered pretty radical at the time. He claimed to have met Manchester United's main firm on a train, that they took him under their wing and that he travelled around the country with them. No, I'm not buying it. It just wouldn't have happened. I know a lot of Man U's Cockney Reds, some of whom he writes about in the book, and they have never heard of him. Perhaps he taught the United boys about nuclear physics in return for them filling him in on their lives as football hooligans.

The exception among the academic books, though, has to be the excellent *Knowing the Score* by Gary Armstrong. A study of Sheffield United fans over a number of years, it is clear that the author really has done his research, unlike previous academic efforts.

In the '80s Colin Ward wrote a book called *Steaming In*, which was a pretty decent account of the era and was certainly the first work that football fans could identify with. Colin was an Arsenal fan who went to Chelsea and England for a couple of seasons. It is obvious that he was there for a while, although by his own admission he was in a strictly observational capacity.

I originally put pen to paper for the first time in my life after reading a series of books by two brothers called Brimson, who seem to have set themselves up as ex-hooligans who want to help rid society of this terrible scourge. The books have sold well, but these two writing volumes on the subject of soccer violence is like me publishing a thesis on line dancing! They hint they were something at Chelsea. No one knew them, and I mean no one. They labour the fact that they were big in the Watford crew. Did Watford have a crew? I never came across it, and I don't know anyone who did. Even if they did have a crew, who are Watford? A punch-up at Hartlepool with five whippet-shaggers hardly qualifies you to write authoritatively about the Millwall, West Ham or Chelsea mobs. They claim that many of the stories they recount are sent in by other hooligans and repeated verbatim. Strange, that, because the style remains constant throughout. The books consist of them preaching about how to save the game from the hooligan menace, their experiences fighting for Watford and these so-called true accounts. They say in their books that they are happy to meet with anyone and stand by their writing. Well, they won't meet with me. I can't get past the researcher on their radio show.

In *Everywhere We Go*, the Brothers Grimm claim to have been there, seen it, done it and bought the T-shirt. Bought the T-shirt, that's about it. In this book they devote a whole chapter, supposedly written by one of their correspondents, to a glassing incident in a pub which received a lot of publicity at the time. They call the section 'Fatman' and it is about a mate of mine, Billy. They harp on about how out of order the incident was and how they were going to slap the people involved. At one point the writer says they were going to use the tube station opposite but didn't because of the CCTV. There was no tube station opposite and no CCTV at the time. They weren't there, they don't know anyone who was there, and as for giving Bill a tug and nearly slapping him . . . silly boys.

In *Capital Punishment* they really give themselves away. They repeat the old myth that Chelsea fans set up a building society account to fund their travel and pay their fines. We've been through that one. Nonsense. Another claim is that Chelsea fans were suspected of burglary and rape, using crime to fund their hooligan activities. I fail to see how rape financially benefits the rapist, but there you go. Chelsea have a right-wing following that dates back to the skinhead era of the late '60s – another quote. Again, untrue. Skinheads in the late 1960s were not racist at Chelsea or anywhere else. They were spawned from the Jamaican culture. Combat 18 are the Chelsea Headhunters. Really? I'm now reaching for my hooligan building society account so I can set off a legal action for libel. And, listen to this one, the police believed that the Headhunters were hiring themselves out to other football firms in need of numbers and, more importantly, scrappers. Can you imagine it?

'Is that Icky? Mickey Francis here – leader of the Guvnors. Could I book three hundred of your finest please for the match Saturday week against United?'

'Sorry, Mickey, we're already contracted with Villa for their match against West Brom. I can probably do you fifty, though.'

'How much?'

'Hundred pound a man, but you pick up any fines.'

'You're on.'

What absolute fucking tosh.

Yet in another offering, *Derby Days*, the Brimson brothers excel themselves. Tony Banks and David Mellor have ignored their offer of advice on how to solve the hooligan problem. Banks and Mellor did not return their calls. Surprise, surprise. They boast about how they set up a 'Supporters United' day to foster good relations and avert violence on the day of a Watford versus Barnet game. Because that's a real flashpoint in the footballing calendar, that one . . .

Talking of Mickey Francis, his book *Guvnors* is about the best I've seen on the subject of football hooliganism. Francis is definitely the genuine article and City did have a tasty firm for a while. I never met up with him but I do recall his brother Donald and the Cool Cats. Sounds like a '60s beat group, doesn't it? Actually it was a '70s beat-up group. Mickey states in his book that Chelsea had the best firm he came up against and his account of a mad Friday night in Manchester in 1984 is honest and true. Mickey's views on the various mobs concur largely with my recollections.

Mobs ebbed and flowed over the years. West Ham, for example, were top in London until Parsons Green (another story) and they haven't really recovered from that. Taking into account the period of time, the numbers and the propensity for violence and disorder, my Premier League would have to be, in no particular order: Chelsea, Millwall, West Ham, Manchester United, Leeds and Cardiff. Clustered together in Division One would be Arsenal, Derby, Newcastle, Tottenham, Everton, Forest, Middlesbrough, Sunderland, Birmingham, Wolves, Portsmouth, Manchester City, Bristol Rovers and Stoke City. The rest are either not really worth talking about or I never saw them first-hand. If they did have mobs, it wasn't for long or they didn't travel far. Although it has to be said that any club can, on its day, pull together teams of nutters for a row. For me, what made Chelsea special was that we always obliged. We weren't always the hardest and didn't always have the biggest numbers, but Chelsea always obliged. No one can deny that. We turned up. Wherever it was. We were always up for the row. Sometimes we ran. But we were always there, and can any other firm honestly say that?

So, has the problem gone? The answer is yes and no. The large-scale punch-ups in and around grounds are gone forever in this country. It is unlikely, therefore, that new leaders will emerge with a countrywide reputation. So the cycle of hero worship and folklore will die off. Some of the old faces have a way to go yet and will still surface now and then, but the cult of the football hooligan as we know it is in its death throes. New boys are not coming through. What remains of the mobs are men over thirty, some as old as fifty and beyond. Because of their very age and experience, the violence is much more immediate and contrived. These blokes haven't got the energy to run up and down backstreets. They need every ounce of strength for the ruck. And the rucks do still happen. Every week, up and down the country. A mobile phone call here, a bit of wasteground there . . . At this point in time they are, finally, the minority. It's now really up to the police and the press. They can keep it going if they like, building the myth, attracting new blood. Or society can say 'enough is enough' and let it die gracefully. We'll see.

Mind you, young men like a fight, and no amount of legislation or hand-wringing can alter that. They are biologically programmed that way. Young men will drink and young men will fight. It stands to reason that semi-organised fighting will rise again somewhere – unless, of course, there is a good war to blast it out of them. Horseracing, maybe? Bank holidays down the coast? Duty-free ferry boats? Vegetarian cooking classes? Anywhere, really. If I were running the country, I would prefer to have it going on somewhere where it could be controlled, keeping it away from peace-loving folk. Football acted as a magnet for those people and those urges. Those people and those urges will always be with us, and now they have been pushed out of football they will find another outlet.

I grew into the world of football gangs and grew middle-aged with them. My youth and early manhood coincided with the rise of the whole cult. From my background I would have been unusual if I hadn't got involved. I was only different inasmuch as it became my main interest rather than merely a passing one. I've met some great and funny people through football and feel richer for the experiences. I don't feel that my exploits in any way make me a bad person. In fact, I think it was the honesty of what we did that unsettled a lot of people. We liked a fight of a Saturday afternoon and we did exactly that with other like-minded people. The rest of the week we got on with our lives. We had a pint, mowed the lawn, washed the car. We didn't lurk in backstreets picking up rent boys or hang from beams with oranges in our mouths and cucumbers up our arses like the people condemning us. I went for the buzz. Every weekend people are seeking the same adrenalin rush by betting on horses, getting pissed, going on manoeuvres with the TA or bungee jumping. Our buzz was deemed illegal, that's all.

The hypocrisy of the condemnation of violence gets on my tits. Violence is rammed down our throats from the day we can first comprehend it. There is hardly a television programme broadcast after six o'clock in the evening that does not contain violence of some kind. The only TV drama we seem to be able to make in this country revolves around police and crime, normally encompassing violence. The big screen is dominated by violence. The news, too. Violence is a staple part of our lives. Yet as a society we affect abhorrence, horror and despair at it. We, on the other hand, don't. We acknowledge that violence is a turn-on and we go out and indulge in it with like-minded souls. That is what I mean about it being the honesty of what we do that frightens people.

Recently I took my daughter to Stamford Bridge. The Shed has been demolished and replaced with tiers and tiers of plastic seats. The atmosphere is still exhilarating but very different. My girl loves it but it is not the same for me. No swaying Shed. No smelly hot dogs. No hoarse cries of 'Zigger Zagger'. Gullit and Vialli have done an Italian job on the team and Zola and Flo are fast replacing Peter Osgood, Charlie Cooke and Alan Hudson in the long-term affections of the Chelsea supporters. I recognise a few people in the seats around me. We've been relegated, us lot, back into the Shed, and soon we won't be able to come in here. The David Baddiels, the Damon Albarns and the rest of the new rich have snapped up our overpriced seats.

I remember now where I've seen the bloke in front of me. It was about twenty years ago and I think it was Ipswich. I'd got split up from the crowd and was winding down some backstreets to find the car. A dozen Ipswich came running around the corner. They stopped and looked at me. I knew I was going to get done, so I tensed myself and said, 'That's right, boys, yes. I am Chelsea.' Out of a newsagent shop had come this bloke. He was on his Jack too. Levi jacket and a cross hanging from his ear. It's gone now, I see. I'd never seen him before in my life, yet he stood next to me.

'Come on, you fucking farmer boys, me and him and you lot.'

The East Anglians ran off and we chased them down the road for good measure. I offered him a lift in our car but he said he'd got a return on the train. I never found out his name and I never saw him again. Until now. He had a thick head of curly hair then. It's thin now, with grey tinges. I'm thinking about tapping him on the shoulder and reminding him of our 1970s encounter when he leaps up following a gratuitous kick on Vialli. He is poking his finger violently in the air whilst effing and blinding loudly. Some stewards, trying to look menacing in their black army jackets and doorman pose, tell him to keep quiet. This makes him worse. Embarrassed spectators inch their backsides away. Two policemen appear from nowhere and attempt to cart him off. All this in seconds. I watch as they lead him away over to the side of the old Shed. I wish I could jump in and help him like he did me all those years ago. But I've got my daughter with me; I think about the job. Rational reasoning. I weigh up one of the stewards instead and fantasise about knocking him out after the game. My old pal struggles and tries to jump into the area where the away fans are, some of whom are taunting him as he is led past. He tries to nut one of the coppers holding him. He's forty if he's a day and he's still up for it.

'Dad,' asks my daughter, looking up at me, 'is that man a hooligan?'

I ponder for a minute.

'Yes, darling, I suppose he is.'

She looks over at a group of youths in front. They haven't even noticed the little drama being played out in front of them. Apprentice beer bellies push out their shiny replica shirts. They're in full song, singing about Vialli.

'Are they hooligans too?' she enquires.

'No, darling, they're fans.'

'And what are you, then, Dad? A hooligan or a fan?'

It makes me think. I pat her on the head and smile.

'I'm a hoolifan.'

Epilogue

It's Millwall again. At the Bridge on a cold winter's night. The 1980s have become the 1990s. The Taylor report, money and the ageing process are ganging up on us boys. Maybe our day has gone but Millwall are here in force and if there is going to be a show it will be tonight. Millwall get on the pitch and taunt the Chelsea boys. Chelsea are unfazed. Excitement is high, as both sets of supporters know it will go off big time outside. The game, whilst exciting, is merely a prelude to the real entertainment to take place in the well-to-do side streets off the King's Road.

Outside the scrapping is everywhere. We're having it with a small Millwall firm and they're pushing us up the Fulham Road, past the garage, towards the Gunter. You can always rely on Millwall. They're getting the better of us although it's equal numbers. It's becoming unpleasant now. A lone figure appears from the shadows. Neatly pressed jeans and a suede jacket. Not a word is said and he is among us. He knows who to punch and does so clinically. Two, now three, go down, and he then carries on walking purposefully towards the ground. He's gone. We all knew who he was. We hadn't seen him for years but he had stepped back into our lives momentarily but effectively. This ghostly intervention freaks the Millwall boys a bit and they back off leisurely across the road. A massive mob appears from around the corner, led by another familiar face. Prison has made his features a touch gaunter but the wide grin, the spiky hair and the bounce in his step are unmistakable.

Football violence lives on, it seems . . .